ORIGINS

CHARLES DORIA is a classicist at large. He has published his own poetry in several journals and anthologies, is the author or editor of four books, and a contributing editor of *Alcheringa: Ethnopoetics.*

HARRIS LENOWITZ is currently Assistant Professor at the Middle East Center at the University of Utah, teaching languages and linguistics. He has published both his own poetry and translations in several journals, and is a contributing editor of *Alcheringa.*

JEROME ROTHENBERG is the author or editor of twenty-two volumes of poetry, including *Poland/1931, Shaking the Pumpkin,* and *Technicians of the Sacred.*

AMS PRESS, INC.
NEW YORK, N. Y.
1976

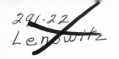

ORIGINS

CREATION TEXTS
FROM THE
ANCIENT MEDITERRANEAN

A Chrestomathy

Co-edited and Translated

with an Introduction and Notes by

LENOWITZ & CHARLES DORIA & HARRIS

With/And a Pre-Face by Jerome Rothenberg

THE AMS PRESS EDITION IS THE FIRST HARDCOVER PUBLICATION OF
Origins: Creation Texts from the Ancient Mediterranean.
AMS PRESS EDITION: 1976

Library of Congress Cataloging in Publication Data
Main entry under title:

Origins: Creation texts from the ancient Mediterranean

Bibliography
1. Creation—Collected works.   2. Cosmogony—
Early works to 1800—Collected works. I. Lenowitz,
Harris. II. Doria, Charles. III. Title.
BL226.074   291.2′2
ISBN 0-404-14849-2
LIBRARY OF CONGRESS CATALOG CARD NUMBER 74-18844

SOME OF THE SELECTIONS IN THIS BOOK HAVE BEEN PREVIOUSLY
PUBLISHED IN THEIR PRESENT OR REVISED FORM IN ISSUES #2,
#4, AND #5 OF *Alcheringa: Ethnopoetics,* COPYRIGHT 1971,
1972, 1973 BY JEROME ROTHENBERG AND DENNIS TEDLOCK;
AND *Alcheringa: Ethnopoetics,* NEW SERIES VOLUME ONE, #1,
COPYRIGHT © 1975 BY THE EDITORS AND BY THE TRUSTEES
OF BOSTON UNIVERSITY; *Io* #6 AND #23, COPYRIGHT 1969
AND 1974 BY RICHARD GROSSINGER; AND *Panjandrum* #4,
COPYRIGHT 1975 BY DAVID GUSS; ACKNOWLEDGEMENT IS ALSO
MADE TO SCRIBNER'S-SIERRA CLUB BOOKS FOR PERMISSION TO
INCLUDE A SELECTION FIRST PUBLISHED IN *Mind in the Wa-
ters,* COPYRIGHT © 1974 PROJECT JONAH; AND TO TREE BOOKS
FOR MATERIAL FROM *The Pirka and the Pearl,* COPYRIGHT ©
1974 BY JEROME ROTHENBERG.

A paperback edition of *Origins: Creation Texts from the
Ancient Mediterranean* is available from Anchor Books.

FOR OUR PARENTS AND CHILDREN
AND TAMAR

This book owes its existence to the support and attention of Jerome Rothenberg and the journal *Alcheringa: Ethnopoetics.* Much of the material in this book first appeared in *Alcheringa,* and the attitudes the journal fosters have helped us form our work. Other individuals and organizations have contributed to the work and aided us. We thank them for their help, without which our *Origins* would never have been born:

The Middle East Center of the University of Utah, its director Dr. Khosrow Mostofi, its faculty and its secretaries, Jennifer Jensen and Lee Snow
The Department of Languages of the University of Utah and its chairman, Dr. Robert Helbling
The Research Committee of the University of Utah
Charles Olson
Richard Caldwell
Albert Cook
David Matlin
Helen Hickerson
James Whitaker
Sigrid Mayer
Robert Callahan and the Turtle Island Foundation
John Clarke and the Institute of Further Studies (SUNY, Buffalo)
Richard Abrams
Charles Sherry
James and Christina Dengate
Michael Doria
David Guss
the ladies of the Sanchez St. Print Shop
Richard Grossinger and *Io* magazine
Madelon Umlauf
our students at the Universities of Utah, Buffalo, and Texas

August 30th, 1974
12th Elul, 5734

CONTENTS

PRE-FACE

What is presented here, these cosmogonies retold, is the paramount interest, & the work of the two who present it is an interest almost equal; & all of it is crucial to the development, the unfolding, changing recovery of cultures & civilizations, that is now to enter its latest phase. Nearly two hundred years have elapsed since that possibility began emerging with the code breakers, the scholars out of Romanticism & driven by the same impulse as its poets, who drew meaning from hieroglyph & wedge, brought the old languages to light—& with those others (searchers & seers again) who needed, demanded, the subterranean & heretical texts that dominant religions & power elites had suppressed for centuries. A historical reconstruction to start with, it was at once more than that: a present concern turned backward, to see the past anew & to allow it to enter into the process of our own self-transformation. "We live," Charles Olson wrote nearly two decades ago, "in an age in which inherited literature is being hit from two sides, from contemporary writers who are laying bases of new discourse at the same time that . . . scholars . . . are making available pre-Homeric & pre-Mosaic texts which are themselves eye-openers."

The gathering that follows has over sixty such eye-openers. Many have never been translated directly into English, almost none (save for an item like the Hittite *Ulikummi,* which Olson himself once handled) into the kind of language that Doria & Lenowitz provide for us here. The change—in the language & structure, the idea in short of what a poem is—isn't peripheral but central, symptomatic of a complex of openings in the aftermath of the two-pronged attack alluded to above. In the paradigm that many of us have come to follow as poets, it's the language that causes us to see, that here can make poetry again from the lifeless things these words were in the first stages of their disinterment. So as the discourse comes to life now in what these two are doing, the past begins to speak through them—at least an image of the meaning & range of the past that no other means could give.

It seems so right here, so alive, that one wonders why it took this long in coming: why, for example, no collection before this had gone back to, translated the available materials around a single topic to provide a "unified field" view of the subject. What happened historically can explain the present situation. Before 1800 our main sources of information for the religion & mythology, the poetry in short, of the ancient world, were classical Greek & Hebrew: Homer & the Bible. Each language had its established works, its canon, & each canon was sufficient to define a classical & sacred tradition: a field for truth & imagination which set the boundaries of reality for man & God. And if our present "curriculum"—whatever classical curriculum remains in schools or on the great books lists—may seem not to have changed much, our actual knowledge has grown through those recoveries that have unearthed & deciphered a score of ancient languages or have revealed alternative traditions in languages already known. Through the nineteenth century & up to the present, specialists have been able to regain & reconstruct much of the poetry of the ancient Near East. And this has led in turn to the publication of poems like the *Epic of Gilgamesh,* the Egyptian *Book of the Dead,* the *Ulikummi,* & the *Enuma Elish:* most in translations that have barely gotten under the skin of the originals or have, as a strategy for recovery of the poem, put it into the language of our conventional & orthodox past.

But for all of that poetic conservatism (& the other conservatisms it has often masked), the historical, mythical, & ethnic realities have continued changing. No longer need one think of Western religion & philosophy as split between two essentially separate traditions: Hellenic & Hebraic. Greek & Hebrew poetry can be read in a new light —shed by literatures older & at least as complex, which paralleled, if not actually influenced, them & which pointed to the existence of an even larger Euro-Mediterranean culture complex. In addition, alternative Greek & Hebrew texts, often outside the established traditions, have continued to come to light: the sacred writings of pagans & gnostic heretics that make an even stronger case for a redefined network of cultural continuities.

Clearly all of this has involved more than pure, disinterested research, as the orthodox defenders, the puritan censors, realized from the start, along with those adventuresome scholars & poets who recognized that the history & roots of our civilization needed to be reexamined & revised in light of the new knowledge. From the latter point of view it was obvious, for example, that such accepted literary forms as epic, drama, history, & so on didn't begin with the Greeks & Hebrews. Not only that, but these categories (the boundaries of which were clearly overlapping) were themselves preceded by an earlier one, the "theogony," & viewed in the light of new concerns with language & function, could be supplemented by forms more in line with contemporary practice: definition, naming, mantra, myth & dream, event & ritual, & so on.

Yet the resistance to popularizing this knowledge was initially widespread: based on prejudices so deeply engrained in the culture that they could hardly be acknowledged until fairly recently. Feelings about Aryan superiority, say, kept many from accepting even the possibility that Homer & Hesiod could have come under Semitic influence —much less the fact. The Greeks had to be narrowly Indo-European or their contribution to Western civilization couldn't be taken seriously. To undermine that uniqueness—blurring long-established distinctions between Jew & Greek—was to strike at the supposed strengths & virtues of Aryan Europe & America.

Religious interests had a parallel stake in maintaining the separateness of the Jewish experience from that of the pre-Christian "nations." And in so far as the scholars were "orthodox" & the texts "pagan" & "heretical," their ideological prejudices hindered translations & studies free from doctrinal & dogmatic preconceptions. In this context it was difficult to empathize with the older texts, to see one's work as part of the transmission of religious & poetic forms that one viewed as superseded or inimical to the "authentic" Christian &/or Jewish revelation. So, for example, many of the "matriarchal" features in pre-Classical & pre-Hebraic literature were treated at best as relics or mere data: even more so when they turned up in Christian works, say, whose initial republication was hedged around by cautionary explications. The puritanism of many of the early editors (or their response to the puritanism around them) also prevented the full & open handling of the erotic & sexual elements in the newly discovered materials—as it had also in long-recognized traditional texts.

Even where much sympathy was present—in Kramer's *Mythologies of the Ancient World,* say, or Pritchard's *Ancient Near Eastern Texts Relating to the Old Testament*—the results, the proof of the work in the poetry, were often ineffective. Almost unconsciously the translators held back, played down their own efforts, as if they were involved in an antiquarian discipline without much interest for the general reader. The language of the translations, the verse itself where verse was aimed at, was too hesitant: the translator as unwilling poet unable to make the leap that would recover the ancient vision & assist the search for primary modes of poetic & religious experience. Or when scholars like Victor Bérard pointed out a community of culture & folkways between Europe & the Near East, their work was dismissed or neglected—this in spite of the use to which Pound & Joyce, say, put Bérard's postulate of a Semitic Odysseus.

But it was among the latter—"contemporary writers laying the bases of new discourse"—that the scope & intensity of the materials were first revealed. Poets specifically & commentators with a less specialized, more universal view of the matter (Olson, Duncan, Snyder, Kelly, Schwerner in his reinvented *Tablets,* Graves & Eliade & Campbell) offered visions of ancient Europes, Asias, Africas, whole worlds united by what Olson called the "pleistocene" or Snyder "the Great Subculture (of illuminati) which goes back as far perhaps as the late Paleolithic." Yet mostly they worked off scattered, bowdlerized translations, taken, *faute de mieux,* at face. The poet's mind supplied the missing force, the linkage: not directly in translation but at a third or fourth remove. The results came first as poems, & that sequence of events may in the long run have set the ground for a new order of translation deriving from the *nous poetikos* as source of energy & form.

The present gathering is a new phase in the process. For the first time the energy enters directly in translation, not as a fluke, an isolated instance, but a full compendium from languages like Hebrew, Greek, Latin, Hittite, Akkadian (Babylonian), Ugaritic (Phoenician, Canaanite), & Egyptian. With their time & place the ancient Mediterranean before the triumph of Christianity & Islam, the editors have concentrated on a central, primal idea, *cosmogony,* the narrative of cosmic origins, & have gathered an unprecedented range of texts around it. These materials aren't taken as philosophy or theology *per se* but as *poesis*: the making or shaping of reality through speech—myth emerging naturally by way of mouth to ear. The narrative here is constantly in the process of defining itself: not the recollection of an ur-text but mind as witness to its own creations.

To bring across this sense of myth as process & conflict, Lenowitz & Doria, working as both poets & scholars, make use of all those "advances in translation technique, notation, & sympathy" developed over the last few decades, from the methods of projective verse to those of etymological translation or of that attention to the recovery of the oral dimension of the poem that the present writer & others have, wisely or not, spoken of elsewhere as "total translation." The picture that emerges is one of richness, fecundity at every turning, from the first image of poem on page to the constantly new insights into the possibilities of "origin." To the latter end the editors offer a wealth of texts never before translated into English (or translated only in relatively inaccessible scholarly publications), along with more familiar texts reinterpreted:* Lenowitz's polyvalent Genesis, for example, or Doria's reconstitution of Empedocles as "magician, weatherman, & raiser of the dead." Hesiod & Homer, Ovid & Vergil, the Yahvist & the psalmists are here seen freshly, surprisingly, as part of a world with rhapsodic, light-struck Orphists, with Pythagoreans mapping out their worlds through numbers, with early Kabbalists exploring alphabetic powers. The work moves from the simplicity of Euripides' ". . . not my story/but one my mother tells" to surreal assemblages of hidden forms & names: the hermaphroditic Elohim & snake/cunt woman of Justin's *Baruch* (leading by stages to the primal god, Priapus) or that recurrent female body-of-the-world qua dragon whom even Yahveh knew. And this allows that "clash of symbols" which, those like Ricoeur tell us, both is natural to mind & forms its one sure hedge against idolatry.

The editors comment little, but go about the more fundamental process of constructing a world of possibilities: not a single sacred

* All work in the anthology has been newly translated by the editors, with Doria concentrating on the Greek & Latin originals, as well as most of the Egyptian, and Lenowitz on those from Semitic languages, Hittite, and the rest of the Egyptian sources. Among the texts that have never before appeared in English are those from Berosos, Abydenos, Pherecydes, etc. In addition the *Enuma Elish* appears for the first time in a full translation as verse, & several works, like Empedocles' *Nature* or those from the Orphists, represent reconstructions from fragmentary sources. Three translations by myself (Apollodorus [Zeus & Typhon], Oppian, & Rabbi Eliezer) represent the only work by a third party.

work of genesis but a space in which all works can come to light. Here the "imaginations of men's thoughts" are no longer the evil that God saw continually but the reoccurring, strangely shifting *gnosis,* reflective of a wider community than heretofore known, with its roots into that older universal shamanism the West would later try to live without. To get this in the open, Doria & Lenowitz let the words (both of their sources & their own) enter again into that process of becoming—as if to begin anew the old work of *formation.*

And that is so much the achievement of this true source book: its great unifying image for poet & general reader alike. It is a presence still, a power & possibility that outlives the terror of its source. In that way the work is never merely literary, never ancient history, but contemporary with all our other works: the very thing we seek in our pursuit of those particulars, even contraries, that open on the universal vision.

Jerome Rothenberg
Center for 20th Century Studies
Milwaukee, Wisconsin
December 1974

INTRODUCTION

We define myth as any widely held account of how something came to be the way it is. This means that in considering any one particular myth of cosmogony we are actually looking at two main aspects: present condition and past event. In this anthology we've collected and translated the most representative creation stories from the ancient Mediterranean area. Instead of reading them as investigations into superseded explanations, let us rather look on them as alternate realities which may or may not correspond to our present sense of ourselves and our experience—to our own myths. They correspond to old or new sciences.

Myth has this value: it unites rather than separates or divides; it provides ways other than the purely sequential to grapple with undifferentiated experience; it preserves instead of eliminating unfathomed reaches and the discoverable/decipherable spaces that make up at least in part the totalities of our existence (i.e., there are mysteries after all; it is not "all there").

Myth involves public ceremonial of some kind. The tribe, the community, celebrates creation in story and rite because if it did not, creation would stop. Everything would fall apart, collapsing upon itself, returning into unspecialized mass: the primes—chaos or egg. The importance of the public act of witnessing and honoring creation is that it lays bare and reconfirms the patterns of the world. This is the true first cause of genesis (if one can speak of the effect as cause in a world where time sails in a circle, where it is difficult to tell beginning from end). The will to exist is the evidence of creation and sets creation in motion.

In the translations that follow we tried not to diffuse what should not only be apprehended as a luminous whole, but participated in.

For the ancients the world lived, it had present reality. The dead returned their life to the living. In turn the dead called the living back to the grave, so that the dead might once again pass out through the gates of life and death. The soul of the earth had to be maintained and fostered by those who inhabited in what the ancients called "regular sequence" (order=cosmos). If it were not, it would revert and become chaotic: viz. our present "present."

Without regular sequence, fish being in the sea, trees in the hills, seasons circling, mind and eye—all these relations that are necessary for other things—would be impossible for these people and poets. Vital interdependence among the myriad creatures would vanish. The cosmos was not seen simple, a sum of all that exists; it was for these scientists as it is for us, the operations and orders that uphold and sway existence. There are, in these operations, two faces or phases. We are in one phase now (the created), but we could easily return into the other (the uncreated) if we do not make adequate provision through our science, our myth, and its transmission.

The will here is human. There is nothing in the nature of things that wants us to make this apprehension. People make connections and predictions and are empowered to keep things going.

In casting about for a suitable explanation for myth-making, particularly for tales of genesis, we constructed the following schema, reading backward, beginning with Memory concerned in such questions as: "How far away is everything?" "Does distance in time equal past or future?" "Where did it go? and will it come back?" If Memory fails in its task of re-connecting, it too will pause and cease. So, to begin, we say the forgotten explanation (that lost chord) is the earliest myth, the first creation, the accounting of the world as experience.

A new fact, a verifiable and repeatable item of knowledge, enters the continuum of Memory; it reshapes the structure, the assembling of experience in ways re-told through Memory. So the first accounting, instantly renewed through story-telling, repeatedly stirs in us an instinct for knowing. It provides the stories Memory uses to make the transition from this present to the real present; from mechanical moment to living time; from first creation to its recurrence in everyone's sense of himself as in—but not of—any time.

In this way our experience of the world, as Olson put it, becomes the "equal of the real." This includes the stories of genesis; how the world got to be the way it is told to us by the created world itself. When the gods create by word, the worlds they summon into being name *them,* not their creations; so there is no one Standard Version for reality and its Masters.

This must be seen by staying clear inside, by annihilating absolute prejudice and dogma. These are the presents of the recent, not the inheritance of real and returning time. By gaining distance on the beliefs of any—this—present, we can bear ourselves as factually assumptive of our own observation.

The stylist of creation story is this vantage, this look-out through time. It shapes the tales of genesis and gives them point. Here we are seeking a cognate for this, a means of reporting experience to the mythic. Effectively cut off from re-telling the world, we are locked into a cell of our own making. We can only stare out through barred windows at a desirable but spurned world, forgetting that it is made out of the same stuff we are (Adam/red-dirt/Terra). But the need to know is present—to be present at one's own making.

We find it necessary to re-state the value of myth in our literalistic culture. For if people haven't changed all that much since 3000 B.C., their world-views have, leaving earlier myths behind as forgotten residue. "Myth" when it is invoked today most often means "falsehood, naïvism" when it introduces an area of previous cultural contract and belief. All myths have as their subject the origin of something: an object, a relationship, an emotion. Even though later generations may (and do) form their own agreements as to how the world began, these agreements lead directly to the necessary formation of some particular "best of all possible cultures," thus obliterating the "truth" of a previous generation's myth. So the particular objective to which people fashion myths will rarely meet successfully the expectations and needs of cultures outside their own, nor will the myth. A myth will always only be understood as true as it reveals the "truth" about those who tell it.

In the case of myths about the beginning of the world (or any collection of myths) we need a canon. If a researcher wants, he can group Hopi myths as distinct from Zuni; he may separate Sumerian stories from Akkadian, or split Roman mythology from Greek. He groups them in convenient ways: by geography, history, or language. The advantages of such groupings are in the first case, to deal with linguistic developments and interchanges; and in the second, to explore the genetic developments of myth from one society to another which neighbors it in time or place. Both sorts of groupings have readily apparent values, corresponding to the diachronic, but there is another, primary way to group them: synchronically, as a corpus of one type (in conjunction with the diachronic classifications listed above). This typology may serve our purposes better because it interferes least with myth-telling itself, and because it allows us more scope for the presentation of the nature of the cultural/personal compact which allows one myth into our schema at a certain point and not another.

The kind of grouping we are talking about relies on a notion Lévi-Strauss re-formulates: "[A myth's] substance does not lie in its style, its original music, or its syntax, but in the story which it tells." This means that myths (as long as they retain quickening power) develop and change what is changeable in them to fit the needs of that time; while what constitutes the variable is whatever a person holding one variant apprehends in another variant as *the same* myth or story.

Lévi-Strauss oversimplifies the case, for "style," "syntax," and "original music" are all integral to the story of the myth, or are each "stories." We think what can best be learned from typological grouping (plus subordination into language, geography, and nationality) is an understanding of ourselves in relation to the original myth-makers and -tellers. How, that is, they felt such arrangements (now viewing the elements in their stories as incidents) became valid through interaction with themselves while rendering an account of the worlds they presently inhabited and to which they gave intelligible life. What we discover from the typology we use are new points of entry into how people think about themselves both in the present (their "now") and the beginnings (their "then").

The movement that characterizes every creation story is toward ever greater elaboration. Beginning with a massive substance within which no single item is distinguishable from any other, lesser units, becoming progressively smaller and smaller, are made distinct. From the ways in which units become discrete other units can be predicted; binding forces on the same level of distinction can be predicted and isolated. As each schema develops it feeds into the complementary schema.

Through this process we gain some understanding of how people conceive the universe: by begetting it first in their own persons, and then trying it out against the world, allowing their worlds and word to set up a process of dialectic we now call "mythopoeia," a dialectic which continues today. In these terms, people describe and participate in their own development of seeing/doing/thinking by active analogy with the universe.

This may be how man's conception of the universe (intellect) develops itself; man describes the development of perception and manipulation. This side-by-side development of the two schemata is certainly the most convincing explanation yet given to the development of intelligence in the individual (see Piaget's *The Construction of Reality in the Child*); man's perception of the creation of the world (myth) is conceived of as man's perception of the development of his own intelligence. Our grouping sheds new light on why creation myths are alike and the ways they define themselves. There is a possibility that this process of side-by-side elaboration of the manipulable universe corresponds to the growth of the infant mind.

The main groupings for this anthology are *creation through word* and *elemental creation*. These seemed the ones our material suggested, not our willful imposition. We observed secondary categories of nationality, language, history, and so forth inside the two main groupings in hopes of making the typology as informative as possible. These categories seem to hold up about as well as any, and, more importantly, do least damage to the stories and even tell us something about creation story itself, over and beyond narrative summaries of individual tales.

By *creation through word* we mean that situation where the god(s) makes any sound—a cough, chuckle, hiss, whatever they emit as separate from themselves—their first emanation. This sound seeks a response; finding it, worlds come into being and take shape, forming basically the name of the god(s). We chose to begin with this grouping not only because it is the one that all poets and storytellers mime in their essential activity, but because through word the first intelligible separation occurs between the maker and the made; cases in which the word serves as the demiurge, the spirit in service of the god's intelligence. It is interesting that Wisdom, appointed the job of creation in one Jewish tradition, says she issued from the mouth of El the Most High before proceeding to her assigned task.

Our second grouping we called *elemental creation* because we noticed how the very things of these worlds (they are usually fire, air, earth, and water) tend to make themselves in various ways and directions, sometimes with, sometimes without the help of gods. The elements themselves in these old stories are animate and divine, the powers of the sensate world. They survive, among other places, in the djinns of Islam. Only a later, more skeptical age stripped them of their numinous presence, converting them into the elements of the scientist's table.

We further broke down this schema into three subgroups: *rising, falling,* and *dividing.* In these categories we notice how the elements associate themselves in various orders—moving up toward their authors/sources or away from them, or continually dividing and therefore multiplying until the Primary of creation had successfully lost itself in the many secondaries of experience.

We decided that *dividing* took place for the most part in two ways: *autonomic* and *aliyan.* By *autonomic* (from the Greek *autos* meaning "self" and *nomos,* "law or custom") we mean that the world laws itself to go on splitting and dividing because that is its chosen condition. And people have recorded that fact about the diacosm in their mythologies. In the *aliyan* group (from a Semitic root *'al* which means "overcoming") we assemble all those creation stories where the world comes into being because of some fundamental split in divinity which goes on repeating itself through history. This split may assume many natures, but almost all revolve around a generational conflict wherein a powerful but decadent first generation attempts to reassert its dominion and its world, sleepy and dark, over a second generation. In such stories the world, as well as present divinity, is renewed and made young by struggle—as for example in the *Sacred Stories* when tyrant Zeus swallows his great-grandfather Phanes only to discover that he becomes a bisexual being, coterminous with the whole world, uniting in his person the scattered contradictions of time. *Aliyan* itself is a standard epithet for Canaanite Baal, El's son and deputy, who creates the world by gaining power over it from outside, a resplendent hero like Marduk-Assur, who slays and dismembers with his light and air the Sea Mother Tiamat, to make earth, air, and sky. The largest number of creation stories fell into this group, which tells us how closely people felt acts of destruction were allied to those of construction. It is the same dipolarity that turns up in Achilles' ash spear that now wounds, now heals.

We placed in the appendix two representative samples of creation through number. These two tales are not really about creation so much as they are expressions of certain underlying relationships between the magic language of numbers and the proportions they evoke in the world. Yet since they re-produce an important method of fashioning the world we felt their inclusion was justified.

In the titles we include as briefly as possible information about the language and site of the myths.

Part One

Creation Through Word

FROM THE SHABAKA STONE

The Shabaka Stone contains a creation story dating back to at least 2700 B.C. Because of its connections with Memphis, "the granary of Egypt," it is sometimes called "The Memphite Theology." Text: K. Sethe, ed. *Dramatische Texte zu Altägyptischen Mysterienspielen,* Vol. 1. "[. . .]" denotes words supplied.

the gods in KHEPERA   of Ptah tree column king
      beetle life maker

Ptah THRONE . . .
    [Isis?]

Ptah NUN   father of ATUM
    water sky   sun disc

Ptah NAUMET   mother of Atum
    counter sky

Ptah Great . . . HORUS and THOTH
      Heart   Tongue
      of the nine [god company]

[Ptah . . . .], - [SETH? . . . . . .] who grew the gods
      [croc pig]
         from under his apron

[Ptah . . . .], - [SHU? . . . . . .] who grew the gods
      [father airs]
         from under his apron

[Ptah . . . .], - [OSIRIS? . . . . .] who grew the gods
      [mummy grain]
         from under his apron

[Ptah . . . .] - [. . . . . . NEPH]THYS lotus
       nurse cup
     flowering on RA'S nose
       sun

Tongue
            in khepera   make body for Atum
Heart

strong   the mouth heart guts right handarm of Ptah!

he grew [the nine god company]
shared himself with [them]
                with their KAS   arms upraised
                        food person double
            Heart   where Horus budded
through   . . . .   of Ptah
            Tongue   where Thoth budded
Heart and Tongue won out over [every other] flesh part
                            ruling the [whole] body
teaching [Ptah] is the [Heart] in the womb body
                the Tongue in the bowl mouth
                of every god man beast worm or thing alive
                    every one

                there [Heart] thinks
                [Tongue] commands
            whatever he wants

the nine god company [of Ptah] stand before him
                grown into bodies of teeth and lips

[teeth are] the water seed
                            of Atum
[lips   ] the lithe spoke arms

lifted from the mouth [of Ptah]
sneezing out SHU   and TEFNUT
            dad airs   ma waters

[his] company of nine grew seeing for eyes
                        hearing for ears
                        breathing for nose

            giving Heart notice

            Heart who lets all thinking rise
            Tongue to say again all [Ptah's] Heart's thought

that's how every god was grown
Atum and his company of nine
yes every god word
      Heart thinks
      Tongue speaks commands
comes true
the kas lived
the hemsets given places
   ka girls
      bringers of food
      hugging into life
through the words
[Heart thought
Tongue spoke]

[justice rewards] them who act for love
[injustice awarded] those whose acts gain hate
life for the peaceful
an ax in the head meaning death
for those who break the peace

this is the way
all work and art
were spoken into life
right handarms gripping weapons
stepping legs
whole bodies wielding limbs
following the command
Heart thought
Tongue spoke
giving everything
meaning that's why
people say
"Ptah seeded Atum in khepera
Ptah made the [other] gods"

he's named Ptah TA-TENEN
          god sneeze grower
flailing them
seated

he talked everything out of [NUN]   into food and feeding
                          [first sea]
feeding the gods and every [other] go[o?]d thing
growing himself stronger
than all of them

peaceful Ptah rested
after he'd done

                          every godword making them true
after he'd spoken

under his fox skin apron
he gave the gods birth
his right eye saw the cities into beetle
his pick dug the canals that water the land
he settled the gods in divine booths
drew up what the rent-food men bring them earns
he hoed their chapels' basements
grew them bellybodies
the likes of which
gave their hearts joy

so the gods entered them into bodies
of [every] wood   metalstone   clay   [other kind of] thing
waxing in lotus from [Ptah godearth dweller]
whose forms they pierced

all the gods
        grew together around [Ptah] peaceful delta sand [?]

all the KAS   Upper Land
                          god lord of the
                                          Lower Land

the GREAT THRONE   barns his grain rejoicing the gods' Heart
    Memphis

    the gods in the [reed?] mansion of PTAH
                              Lady of all [   ] life
                              who gives [the wheat]
                              bolstering both Lands

when his water drank OSIRIS
                    grain eye
wife ISIS
      throne
                    watched
sister NEPHTHYS
         cup house

they saw
grief carved them

               Isis
HORUS told   :
hawk   Nephthys
                    "don't wait   grab
                    get my father out of his water"

the women moved their heads in time
they let him land

Osiris went through the hidden door five cobras guard
into the lion coiled luxury of the eternal lords
where the sun cock shines
                    rays perpetually corded
growing walking
along Ra's high road
falcon head god sitting
wearing the snake wrapped sun
at GREAT THRONE
    Memphis
         enrolled at the gala court
Osiris
         ranked among the gods
              of Ptah TA-TENEN   lord of years
                    god grower

FROM THE *PYRAMID TEXTS*

This particular creation story from Passage 600 of the *Pyramid Texts* was found cut in stone inside the pyramids of Mer-ne-Re and Pepi II (Sixth Dynasty—c. 2400 B.C.). Text: Sethe, *Die Altägyptischen Pyramidentexte.*

say in serpent body

                :

"ATUM   KHEPERA
  sun disc   beetle life maker

             you climbed the top of pyramid hill
making the light the *bennu* bird phoenix recurring sun gives
in god bird house ON   over universe water bowl
       SunTown
where you shoved out Shu
     spat out Tefnut
           spittle from your lips
           asp rippling waves of the mouth

       putting arms around them
            clasped them
     in your KA
         double person food

        having them share
      the ageless soul disposed in you

. . .

ha! strong nine god company in On—

        SHU
        daddy airs

        TEFNUT
        ma waters

        GEB
        lord earth

NUT
lady sky

OSIRIS
mummy fucker

ISIS
cunt river

SETH
sage pig

NEPHTHYS
nurse cup

ha!   Atum Khepera spit named 'Nine Bows' in On
you who never back away from him
offer your heart's shelter . . .

and Atum—protect
protect from all gods from all dead . . ."

FROM *GOD|gods*

From *GOD|gods*, a Greek text written in Egypt probably by a heterodox Jew sometime before the third century A.D. It forms part of a long *lysis* (a ritual of purificatory "loosing" that took about fifty days to complete) from an older native magical tradition. Text: Papyrus XIII in *Papyri Graecae Magicae* (Preisendanz, ed.), Vol. II.

. . .

say   :

" YOU

Who sees one and all
Who no one sees

I'm calling YOU
biggestbest GOD
All Maker
Your Own Father-Mother-Child

giving Sun the glory of his blaze and every strength
ordaining Moon wax and wane to keep her paths straight
taking nothing from the darkness born before they were
YOU dealt all equal shares

when YOU appeared splendid in light
the universe was authored
from that brightness
coming into view

all in all subjects itself in order
to   under YOU :

Metamorph : Capable-Of-Every-Form

Whose true body

the gods have never seen

I want YOU : Invisible Time outlasting time
right here

Kyrie/Lord
in good body for me to see

since I slave beneath Your world for Your Angel :
　　[name]　*Bi-ath-yap-bar*

　ber-bir　　　*schhih-lah-tour*　　*bou-fhroum-trohm*

　　　　　　　　　　　　　　for Your Fear :
[names] *Dha-nouf*　*Hhrah-tor*　*Bel-bali*　*Bal-bith,*
　　　　　　　　　　　　　　Yah-woh

　　　YOU
　　　　　Who made heaven and earth
　　　　　　　　　stand up together

　　　YOU I want
　　　Kyrie/Lord
　　　　　right here

since it's from GOD
　　　　　gods take sight
　　　　　　　to start their doing
　　　　　　　using *Ech-he-bu-crohm*/Strength-of-Sun
whose shining-prayer-in-praise-of is :

a	*a*	*a*
e	*e*	*e*
o	*o*	*o*
i	*i*	*i*
a	*a*	*a*
o	*o*	*o*

　　　Sha-ba-oth
　　　Zha-gou-reh
　　Ar-bath-Yah-Woh
　　　god *Arathu*
　　　　Adoni

                    I'm telling YOU
                                right here
                            Kyrie/Lord
                        I want YOU

                    named in bird :
                            arai

                    in hieroglyph :
                            laïlam

                            Hebrew :
                            anochh / I am

Bi-ath-yar-bath   *ber-bir*   *ech-hi-lah-tour*
                                            bhou-froum-trohm

                        Egyptian :
                            Aldabahim

            like the dog-faced baboon :
                            Abrasax

            the sparrow hawk :

khi   *khi*   *khi*   *khi*   *khi*   *khi*   *khi*   *tif*   *tif*   *tif*

                        in priest :
                            me-ne-foh-if-oth

    ha   *ha*   *ha*   *ha*   *ha*   *ha*   *ha*

                    now [child] :
                CLAP   *CLAP*   *CLAP*

        go :
            TSWEEEEEEEEEEEEEEETSEETSEETSEEE

SSISSISSISSISSISSISSISSISSISSISSISSISSISSISSISSISSISSISSISSISSISSISSI

```
                come to me
               Perfect Lord
             Who knows no pain
            Who pollutes no place
                  why?
                because
                  GOD
          I have been Completed by
                 and so
                I Know
                 Your
                 Name
                 ————
                        ”
```

[A week of preparation follows. This includes building an altar outdoors with a tabernacle tent. On the eighth day:]

in the dead of night during the 5th hour
when everything is still
go to the altar of sacrifice

light the candles

put beside it two chickens and two oil lamps ¼ full
(you won't need more than that)

recite the prayer and the GOD-mystery
which is called "scarab the shit beetle"

set out a mixing bowl filled with black cow's milk
and wine without sea water

for this is beginning and end/
drink-offering and sacrifice-eating

write the prayer on both sides of a tablet of natron [*nether?*]

lick one side clean

soak the other in water and wash it in the mixing bowl

use ink of perfume and flowers

before drinking the milk and wine
perform out loud the prayer that follows

then lie down on a mat and listen

pen and tablet in hand do :

" *The Prayer-Hermes-Does*

I'm calling YOU
whole world in Your hands
! ! !   OVER HERE   ! ! !
speaking in all voices and tongues
just as they sang in glory for YOU
that first time
when the world began
for words are Your doing
we believe they are
absolutely true
because YOU are

:

Helios
Sun
[name]   *Ahhebucrom*
meaning——'flame leaps from
Your Disk
like wheelspokes'

I give YOU praise
opening :

a   *a*   *a*

e   *e*   *e*

o   *o*   *o*

YOU made air burst into full
from sunblaze
the stars' white bodies
stand up night
when YOU built and peopled
of light of god
the ordered world

i   *i*   *i*

a   *a*   *a*

o   *o*   *o*

when YOU
[names] :   *Shabaoth*
Arbath-Yah-Woh
Zagoureh
made the world
distinct and clear

Your angels
who came first to light
are named
Arath
Adoni
Ba-shemm
Yah-Woh

Arath cries out in bird
'arai!'
meaning——'pain and woe on those I hate'
YOU put him in charge of the *Timoriai*
Enforcers of Your wrath

Sun sings in glory to YOU in priest
:   *'Laïlam'*
in Hebrew with the same name

: anok (I am) :
Bi-ath-yar-ba(r)-ba(r)-ber-birsh—shi   *la-tour-bouf-froum-trom*
(36 letters)

meaning——'I am leading the way for YOU, Lord

ThankYOU I am *Helios* SunDiskgod
getting out of my flat barge'

now in hidden I spell
Your natural name
in Egyptian:
A
   l-
     d
       a-
         b
           i-
             a-
               hi
                 m
(nine letters
going down)

now getting out of Sun's flat barge
wrapping himself in light for eyes is
dogheadfox

he greets YOU with :
'Abrasax = year's number
that's Who YOU are hello'

now leaving the other side of the barge is
sparrow hawk
he greets YOU and
cries for food :

_hi_   _hi_   _hi_   _hi_   _hi_   _hi_   _hi_   _pippippip_   _pippippip_

Ennead/Company of Nine
say good-day to YOU in priest
'_Me-nef-ho-if-hoth_'
meaning——they're saying   :
'Lord, I lead the way for YOU'
"

END   PRAYER
****

(break)

then :

CLAP   _CLAP_   _CLAP_

go ahead
do it

GOD
laughed
seven
(7)
times :

_HA_   _HA_   _HA_   _HA_   _HA_   _HA_   _HA_
_HA_   _HA_   _HA_   _HA_   _AH_   _HA_

FROM THE *HIDDEN SACRED BOOK*
OF MOSES CALLED "EIGHTH" OR "HOLY"

Like *GOD|gods*, this is a Greek text written in Egypt probably
by a heterodox Jew. It contains a different version of the tale
of GOD's Seven Laughs, longer than the one found in
GOD|gods. Text: Papyrus XIII in *Papyri Graecae Magicae*.

the 7 Laughs of GOD
Hha   Hha   Hha   Hha   Hha   Hha   Hha

each Laugh HE gave
engendered the 7
god   god   god   god   god   god   god
the Fore-Appearers
who clasp everything one

first Laugh
PHOS(AUGE)   showed up
Light(Flash)

                        All splitter
                        born universe god
                                fire god

second Laugh
HUDOR filling everywhere
Water

                        he echoed
                        Earth heard
                        she saw AUGE
                                Flash
                        she was afraid
                        and writhed
            the HUGRON waving tender smooth
                the Wet

GOD cut in threes
       three lots
       three destinies

            a new god took light

            whom GOD arranged
            to rule water's pit

            so unless this god helps

            HUGRON won't grow
            Wet

            bigger or smaller

            tides billow
            and curl up

WaterMaster's
named :

Prom-sach-ha   Al-eh-eh-i-oh

    for you are

O - e - a - i
    be-thel-leh

third Laugh
GOD wanting to

appeared from HIS rage
NOUS(KAI PHRENES)
Mind(and Brains)

given a heart

his name:
Hermes

translates the diacosm's totals
interprets whatever is

in charge of Phrenes
he manages

he is the steward
of universe house

of course he is:
She-meh-shi-lamps

fourth Laugh

apparent self   GENNA
                FuckMakeBabies

                      witnessing she is strong
                      over everything's sperm

                      all that's seeded
                      turned a parent

                      thanks her
                      named :

                Ba-day-to-foth   *Zoh-thaks-at-hoh-dsoh*

fifth Laugh
GOD smiled wept
showed in light MOIRA
                Lot-Portion

                      holding a balance beam

                      meaning in her
                      justice is minded

                      Hermes argued said:
                      "she's got my job"

                      they quarreled
                      GOD came out:

                      "what is right you
                      two bring to light

                      but all in the universe
                      will stand under you"

first to take the scepter
                of creation

        she is named
                in holy

        anagrammed
        because so
                fearful

        it makes you
                shudder

            it is

    thaw-ri-ow-bri-tih and so on

(her name in anagram
is bigstrong
holy
all honor it everywhere
yes a much name
strength name:

thaw-ri-ow-bri-tih-tam-mah-ohr-rang-ah-doh-
i-oh-dang-ar-roh-am-mah-tir-boy-roth,

                        49 letters)

sixth Laugh

made HIMself joyous

KAIROS   turned light
ModeSeason

carried a rod
meaning KingMastery

handed it
to [Phos]
god light
built first

who took it
said:

"let yourself enter
the globe of hoped-for glory
of PHOS
Light

and be next
to me
because before anyone else did
you gave me the rod that rules

whatever was
and likely will
you stand over"

after heshe went into the sphere of Light
the SunDisk
who spins in center
around himself
displayed an airbreath of Phos

GOD said to queen [Kairos?]
"all right
be englobed
in that airbreath

stay with Phos
hold everything
in circling embrace

grow through Light
take and stop taking
from him

you help
and whatever is
waxes wanes"

[Kairos'?] bigstrong astonishing name :

"anagh (*I am*) :
Bi-ath-yar-bar   ber-bish-hi-la   tour   bou-froun-trohm"
(36 letters)

seventh Laugh

wheezed while HE did it

bore PSYCHÉ
SoulBreath

everything got moving

GOD said:

"you'll keep them that way
on the move

and happy
when Hermes gives you the road"

HE stopped talking
they all started moving
each along their road
Living Wind bellying them
and
there's no
stopping them

GOD looked
HE went

pepepepepepepepepepepepepepep

just like a bird

startle
scaring everyone

PHOBOS   dressed in light
ScarePanic

full armed armored
god named:

Danoup   Hhrator   Berbalih   Balbithih
                              (26 letters)

then He bowed beckoned to Earth
gave a big

SSHHSSHHSSHHSSHHSSHHSSHHSSHH

snake's tone

she caught HIS note
opened her womb neck
bore special child Pythian Python
who knows about things
                    before they happen
thanks to the piercing snakesound GOD made

Python's big holy name:

Ilillouih

I-lil-lou-ih

I-lil-lou-ih

i-thor

marmaraugeh

foh-hhoh

foh-boch

after Python showed
Earth doubled up
reared up
pranced

Sky Axle held still
although portioned
to come with her
moving his stick
              in her time

24   ORIGINS

GOD said:
        "Yah-Woh!"

everything stopstood

rose in light
[Yah-Woh]
big god biggest
standing things
in the universe
before now
and later

no longer
did any aerial mists
of heavenly lands
get mislaid
out of order
no way

Phobos saw
askedknew:
        "Yah-Woh stronger than me?"

stood against him
butted
"I was here before you"
rebutted
"I stood everything"

GOD said:
"Phobos you are the child
             of a bird call
he of snake hiss
        a better noise
            than made you
yet from you two will come
when you show up later
power to make all things stand
the way they're allotted"

Yah-Woh's named

Danoup   Hhrator   Berbalih   Balbith,   Yah-Woh

GOD chose to offer aslant
honor to the god [Yah-Woh]

standing aside with HIM

so when he showed
GOD gave him the nine gods
to lead in front
holding equal
power and glory

HE called their nine distinctions
named the horn tips of their names:
"Bosbeadii"

and the seven planetstars:

a	e	e	i	o	u	o
e	e	i	o	u	o	
e	i	o	u	o		
i	o	u	o			
o	u	o				
u	o					
o						

o	u	o	i	e	e	a
u	o	i	e	e	a	
o	i	e	e	a		
i	e	e	a			
e	e	a				
e	a					
a						

(bigstrong amazing anagram)

biggestbest one's HIS name
that strong one
27 letters

Abohrch   braohch   hhrammaohth   Yah-Woh

putting it another way:

Abrohch   braohch   hhrammaohth   prohap   bathoh
Yah-Woh   o   u   a   e   e   i   o   u   o

FROM THE *POIMANDER*
OF HERMES TRISMEGISTOS

A Greek revision of an earlier Egyptian cosmology, c. A.D. 100.
Text: Nock, trans., Festugière, ed., *Corpus Hermeticum,* Vol. 1,
1–19, 30–31.

One day I started thinking about what was real; my mind had
gone from me to so high a place my senses ceased. Sleep weighed
me down, just as if I had eaten too much or overworked. I
saw a Great Man (how big he was, I couldn't tell, but he was
enormous) coming toward me. He called my name and said:

"What do you want to hear and see? And learn and know
                              through thought?"

"Who are you?"

"I am Poimander Men'sShepherd Mind of Authentia Absolute Master.
I know what you want to do. Wherever you are I am."

"I'd like to find out what is real—and how it came to birth.
I want to know god."

"Think. And I will teach you."

then he changed the way I saw him
I looked inside him and found
he'd opened every thing for me to see
in a downward turning.

an infinite vision overcame me
light born(e) wherever I turned
                    light calm clear laughing gently full
I watched I loved

Afterward I saw the darkness that silts toward the bottom
                              squatting in her corner
begin raining her somber face
spiraling out like a (snake) sidewinding her coils

                    then she seemed
            to change into a water shaken from within
                from depths beyond telling
then smoke as if she held inside her (unseen) fires
returning echoes trebly pitched chiming notes sadder than words

she screamed what no "a," "an," or "the" could give sense to
hissing and crackling like a voice of fire

out of the light . . .
holy Word plunged into this BirthWorld Darkness

clear fire leapt from Water up into the high
bursting with act
lightly piercing my eye

Air of Light
chased this FireWind
she closed herself up under him
                    mounting above Earth and Water
which makes it seem she hangs onto him

Land and Sea stayed below where they were
mixing/mingling each other
impossible to tell one from the other
stirred by the Wind'sWord born(e) within earshot against them

"Do you know what you saw?"

"I will"

"I am Light your god Mind
who gave myself to sight
before DarkWater's birth
the glowing Word Mindvoiced
is god's son"

"And then?"

"Know
what hears in you and sees
is the Word of the Lord

your mind the FatherGod

Father and Son are One
this makes life

now turn towards the Light
and understand"

he stopped talking and looked me straight in the face for so
long I started shaking. That was when

he raised his head
I saw in my mind
the Light born in countless powers
bear the infinite ordered world

the Fire hemmed in everywhere by the strongest power
still stood in place

all this   in my mind
while I looked inside at the world
through Poimander's Word

I was still lost inside ecstasy
when he spoke again

"you see in your mind the seeming that starts type
beginning the beginning
of the beginning that never stops"

"where did the rows/the L M Nts of birth come from?"

"from god's intention
once it has taken Word
and sees the lovely World of Birth

she remembers to execute by heart
whatever he says
setting herself in order through the rows of birth
and the SoulBreaths, their first yield

god the malefemale Mind Life Light the first being and doing
bore by Word Worker Mind 2 the fire/wind/god
who worked up from scratch seven Comptroller Stars
who fold their circles around the world strained
                                        to human notice
they call their Accounts *Heimarmené* : Lot-Payment

immediately god's Word bounded away
                        from the downward bearing (birth) rows
towards that light-scoured workfact named BirthWorld
making himself one with Worker Mind 2
for they enjoyed the same birth
leaving behind the crazed wordless sloping L M Nts
to furnish unwrought subject things

Worker Mind 2 with Word
enclosed the (Stars') circles
holding on to their buzzing cones
he made these workfacts of himself wheel on their own
                        right from a start without beginning
towards an undetermined end that never stops
for (the Stars') bearings end where they begin
giving birth as willful Mind permits
to the crazed Wordless lives
of those the stooping rows of birth inform

air brings forth those that fly; water those who swim

land and sea split
cutting away from each other differently

the Earth had four-footed and creepingcrawling children
the animals tame and wild

All Father Mind Light and Life
bore Anthropos the Great Man to be his image
whom he fell so deeply in love with
because the childMan was his
Anthropos the Lovely
no matter how you looked at him was
Dad's true mirror

when Mind discovered love outside himself
in fact in his (son's) bodyform
he gave him sovereignty
over all the creatures Worked from Thought

when the Great Man saw
what Worker Mind 2 had done with Fire
he wanted that gift for himself

his Father agreed

Anthropos fathered himself
inside Worker's Sphere
where he was to be absolute lord
the Comptrollers fell in love with him
they gave him each
a share in their power

once he learned who they are
and had enjoyed their birthrights
he wanted to shred their circles' sheltering limit
to find out for himself
how strong he who sits on fire and rules it is

Anthropos
who now held all there is of the appointed world of the dying
of those who live mindless/wordless
cast his bent below (the Stars') harmonious windings
tearing apart their cunted shell
he showed falling BirthWorld god's lovely body

she saw he owned in him beauty
and all the (Stars') energy
while his body formed Fathergod's mirror
she gave him a smile for Eros/Love
for she'd seen her oceans reflect
                              his supreme loveliness
which sometimes shaded her earth

he too had seen her seem
to borrow his shape in the water
and loved her for that
planning to make her house his home
will gave him the strength
to plunge into her silly wordless box
BirthWorld opened taking him in
enlacing her beloved
inside her sheer Wholes
they mixed and mingled
they loved each other

which is why
of all who live on earth
it's only people
who compound twice in doubt

I mean they either die through body
or else live without death
        through Anthropos who appears the way he is

for while everyone is immortal
and has   power over all things
they still suffer death's enclosure
                subjecting themselves to Lot-Portion

and although (born) beyond the Stars' pinched wheels
they enslave themselves making the heavens their Paymaster

once true malefemales
                because their father was
and tireless

FROM THE "POIMANDER" OF HERMES TRISMEGISTOS   33

because heshe never needed sleep
. . . (they wind up)   defeating themselves"

"I too love Word"

"what I tell now is the Secret hidden until this day

after BirthWorld slept with Anthropos
she did something almost unbelievable

since the Great Man had shared
half by Fire half by WindSoulAir
in the birthrights of the Seven Comptrollers
                          and their fixed symmetry
she did not wait
she immediately sluiced out of her funnels

seven malefemales (moving) high above this world
mockmiming the original Stars"

"more"

"Silence. I have not finished beginning

The first people were born like this
first there was Girl Earth
then FuckFather Water

Fire made them ripen

then BirthWorld took Windsoul(s) from FireAir
and bore bodies that looked like the Great Man's

Anthropos of Life and Light
reproduced himself
changing his Life to Soul
                 Light to Mind

staying that way
(he became) every(breathing/thinking) thing
                    in the apparent world
until time closed one cycle
and the moment of birth into species began

listen closely: this is what you've been waiting for

when that moment came around
(Father)God willed the chain that binds one and all
to let go

every living thing that (up till then) was malefemale
untied

dissecting into sex
even the people

some breaking into men
others women

Immediately (Father)God spoke to them in holy Word:
'grow in your growings
fill by filling
all of (Worker Mind's) FactMadeThings

be minded
know yourself
            means you will not die

the only way you can do that
is to love

find out about everything that is'

After God spoke his ForeThought
            worked through Lot-Portion
            and the Stars' tightly-meshing wheels
she manipulated the sexes' mingling
building their generations from below

everything prevailed in multiples of kind

all who know they will not die
reach that gentle goodness
                which is everywhere

those who love the body
                the child of vagrant love
remain below and roam the ShadowWorld
                        in deep pain
            because death's business
                    concludes their sensings"

. . .

this is why I made a song of praise
with all my strength and soul'sbreath
for Father God:
"Blessed is God
        Father of the Wholes
            Whose powers execute his will
                Who wishes to Know
                    and be Known by
                        His own
            Who gave by Word
                        everything that is
                        understanding
            Whose image all BirthWorld bore
            Whose body/shape
                she did not change
            Who stronger than His every power
                rules over the high and mighty
            Master of those who praise Him

receive the pure word sacrifices of my soulbreath
                and heart stretched to the limit towards You
                The Uninvocable
                The unnameable
                        Spoken-Only-In-Silence"

PRIESTLY GENESIS

The cosmogony of the Hebrew P Document, Genesis 1.1–2.4a,
c. 550–450 B.C. Text: Kittel, *Biblia Hebraica.*

At the first of the gods' godmaking skies and earth, the earth was
all mixed up—darkness on top of deepness; so the gods' spirit swooped
down on the waters.
　　The gods said LIGHT　　so there was light, and the gods liked the
light so they made it different from the darkness:
　　　　　　　　they called the light Day
　　　　　　　　called the darkness Night;

　　　　　　　　so that was Evening
　　　　　　　　and that was Morning
　　　　　　　　the first Day.

　　Then the gods said, LET A SPACE BE BEATEN OUT,　and
it was TO SPLIT THE WATERS UNDERNEATH IT FROM THE
WATERS ON TOP OF THE SPACE.
　　　　　　　　the gods called the space Skies

　　　　　　　　so that was evening
　　　　　　　　and that was morning
　　　　　　　　the second day.

　　Then the gods said, LET THE WATERS-BENEATH-THE-
SKIES BE GATHERED TOGETHER INTO ONE GROUP SO
THE DRYNESS CAN BE SEEN.
　　And they were.
　　　　　　　　the gods called the dryness land
　　　　　　　　called the gathering-together-of-the-waters seas.

　　　　　　　　The gods liked what they saw
so they said
　　　　　　　　SPROUT THE EARTH SPROUTS:
　　　　　　　　GRASS SEEDING SEEDS
　　　　　　　　TREES MAKING FRUIT,
　　　　　　　　FRUIT ITS SEED IN IT,
　　　　　　　　EVERY KIND ON EARTH.

So it was like that; the earth brought out sprouts: kinds of seed
seeding grass, kinds of seed-in-fruit-making trees
        and the gods liked it.

        so that was evening
        and that was morning
        the third day.

Then the gods said, LET THERE BE LIGHTS IN THE SPACE
OF THE SKIES TO SET THE DAY OFF FROM THE NIGHT.
THEY'LL BE MARKING TIMES, DAYS AND YEARS, AND
THEY'LL BE LIGHTS IN THE SKIESPACE LIGHTING THE
EARTH.

So that's how it was: the gods made the two big lights: the
bigger light for running the day and the littler light to run the night
with the stars.

        the gods presented them
        in the skiespace
        to light the earth
        to run day and night
        to make a difference
        between the light and the darkness

        and the gods liked it.

        so that was evening
        and that was morning
        the fourth day.

Then the gods said
        SWARM WATERS SWARMS
        BREATHING LIFE
        AND FLYERS FLYING
        OVER THE EARTH
        OVER CROSS SKIESPACE

so the gods godmade big sea beasts, and all breathing crawling life
on Earth; the waters swarmed and all the birdwing
        and the gods liked it
        and blessed them:

BREED A LOT, AND FILL
THE WATERS OF THE SEAS
AND THE FLYER MAKE MANY
ON THE EARTH.

so that was evening
and that was morning
the fifth day.

Then the gods said, LET THE EARTH BRING OUT
BREATHING LIFE OF ALL SORTS: CATTLE AND
CRAWLER, EVERY EARTH LIFE
and that's how it was:
Gods made all earth life
cattle and red-dirt crawler too
all of all kinds
and liked it
so the gods said
LET'S MAKE SOME RED DIRT THAT'LL
LOOK LIKE US,
JUST LIKE US
IT'LL BOSS:
THE FISH IN THE SEA
THE BIRD IN THE SKY
AND CATTLE
AND ALL THE EARTH
AND ALL THE CRAWLERS CRAWLING
THE EARTH
so the gods
godmade man as he looks
looking like the gods
they godmade them
prick and hole
they godmade them

and the gods blessed them
and the gods said to them:

BREED A LOT AND FILL THE EARTH
AND TAKE IT OVER.
RULE:

THE FISH OF THE SEA
THE FLYER OF THE SKIES
ALL LIFE THAT CRAWLS ON THE EARTH.

Then the gods said
HERE WE'VE GIVEN YOU:
EVERY SEED SEEDING SPROUT
OVER CROSS THE WHOLE EARTH,
EVERY TREE BEARING FRUIT
SEEDING SEED
FOR FOOD,
FOR YOU;

AND FOR EVERY:
LIFE ON EARTH
FLYER OF THE SKIES
CRAWLER ON THE EARTH
BREATHING LIFE,
EVERY GREEN SPROUT
FOR FOOD.

and that's how it was

and the gods liked everything they saw
very much
so that was evening
and that was morning
the sixth day.

Now the skies, earth, and all their troop were complete. The gods
finished off all the work they'd done on the sixth day, and rested on
the seventh day from all the work they'd done.

The gods blessed the seventh day,
set it apart,
because they'd rested on it
after all the works
the gods had godmade to work.

That's the story of the godmaking of the skies and earth

"WISDOM" FROM *ECCLESIASTICUS*

From *Ecclesiasticus*/Ben Sira, a Hebrew text of the second or third century B.C., Pharisaic. Texts: Vulgate, Septuagint, Levi—*The Hebrew Text of the Book of Ecclesiasticus*. Ecclesiasticus 24.3–12a.

(Wisdom speaks of herself)

"I came out of El's mouth   first
   flooded across the earth
then built my home high
        my seat in cloud pillar

I was alone   traveling the circle of Sky
        going back and forth through Tehom-deeps

I held seawave and all the earth
    every people and nation
                seeking rest with all
'Whose home can I stay in?'

The One who made everything assigned me
The One who made me set my stay:
              said
'Stay with Jacob
Set yourself in Jerusalem'

He made me   starting   before the world
I do not stop   ever
I served in the Tent
then set in the Temple
I stayed in the Holy City
            the power of Jerusalem
I rooted in the Chosen People"

THE SEVEN DAYS OF GENESIS
FROM THE *SECRETS OF ENOCH*

From *The Book of the Secrets of Enoch,* a Hebrew-Greek-Slavonic text, c. first century B.C. Text: Charles and Morfill, *The Book of the Secrets of Enoch.* "(*B:* . . .)" indicates alternate readings from B version; "(. . .)" indicates suppositions; "(. . . ?)" indicates guesses; "???" indicates lost words; "***" indicates approximate sense, syntax corrupt.

God speaks to Enoch face to face

"Enoch—sit beside me
on my left with Gabriel"
I knelt in front of him

"Enoch whom I love—
I tell you that
everything you see
that stands complete
from before it began
I made (taking)
all that you see
from what you do not
from that which is not

hear what I have not told
my angels who don't know
how they began or why
my kingdom never ends

who haven't heard
how I opened light
and rode inside
like a ghost
like Sun when he visits east to west
yet lives in peace with himself

for I did not
when doing everything
I conceived the thought of creation
putting a floor under it
letting everyone see
what I had done
the bottom of dark

I called down to the deep below
'come from the unseen dark
all that eye can see
Adoïl—come'

he came hauling so large
a stone of light it made
his belly a giant ball

'explode—Adoïl
push out the light
give it birth'

he blew out the stone
light gaping his belly womb
opening all I willed for shape

light the mother of light
bore a great age
the star heaven
which I saw was good

(where)
I built a chair
and sat down

then :
'light—rise
above my throne
take body as home
for the highest (stars)'

I leaned back on my seat
and looked up
above light
there is nothing

the bottom once more

again I called
to the darkness you cannot see
'come—Archas
heavy stiff and deeply red (*B:* black)
tear bright firm body
from the unseen (wavering dark?)'

he lived up to my word

'Archas—undo (your belly womb)'

he shook loose from his hollows
(earth realm)
an age I saw was good
big black mother
rearing the make
of all who live in her

'Archas—go down (to her)
house in your body
the lower world'

which he did

(under Archas)
below dark
there is nothing

water circled with light planted on seven islands

I said
'???—come from light and dark
thicken shape'

and ??? happened

which I layered in sheets with light
and set down for a road

this is how water
a path below light
spread over shadow
was born

bottomless water
who I made take body

who I embraced in seven glowing disks
(one inside the other)
working in concentrics
outward towards the last

who I drew of such crystal
that is wet and dry
glass pictures it

every root I showed a path
water I told
'ebb and flow
your way'

I set the seven stars
in the sky each a track

all this
I saw was good

light and dark
scampering in water
I made differ—
to the light
'you are day'
to the dark
I said
'you are night'

evening and morning : the first day

the week of God
his wisdom and power every moment all those seven days
the strengths of sky earth's might
everything that moves
meaning men and women too

THE SEVEN DAYS OF GENESIS   45

into the sky's disk
I put body
water I compelled into one
draining the confusion between wet and not-wet
the big rocks grown from water
I heaped up
I cut of fire
ten squads of immaterial stars
my angels Cherubim Seraphim Ophannim (etc.)
who dress in
whose weapons are flame
my advice to them
'each one
keep to your ranks'

Satanaïl and his angels thrown down from the high place

one did not
he turned away
taking his band

he mothered a thought without force (or: that could never reach act) :
to lift his chair above the clouds sheathing earth
equating himself to me

I threw him down

Satanaïl flew through the air
above the abyss
and didn't stop

(evening and morning :)

the third day

before starting the living
and feeding them
I said to earth
'grow trees big with fruit
shoot up grass hills
and every seed for sowing'

I planted Paradise Park
and walled it off
armed fire angels
standing guard

I made earth spring
and gave her this law
'do it over and over again'

evening and morning :

the fourth day

I ordered fires (for the cone)
of the sky's circles

for the first and highest : the (biggest) stars (and)
                                            Kruno (Kronos/Saturn)
for the second : Aphrodit (Venus)
the third : Aris (Ares/Mars)
(? the fourth : ???)
fifth : Zeus (Jupiter)
sixth : Ermis (Hermes/Mercury)
seventh and lowest : Moon ordering her way
                                 elegantly with the smallest stars

in the bottom ring
I stationed Sun
to light up day
Moon and (smallest?) stars
to provide for night

my orders for the sun
'journey with each zodiac beast
until (you've matched with all) twelve'

I told month
to follow month
until (they'd reached) twelve
I gave them
names lives thunder-seasons
marked hours
drew lines
for them

evening and morning :

the fifth day

I said to the sea
'make the kinds you can
of fish
of bird of feather
all who creep
and walk on earth
who fly through air
(sex them)
male and female
every soul drawing life's breath

(*B:* then I told [Achamoth] my Wisdom
to make man for me)

evening and morning :

the sixth day

I told (Achamoth) my Wisdom
'give me a male-sex man
of seven standings :
of flesh of earth
blood of rain
eyes sun
bones rock
mind from angels' wing and speeding cloud
veins (nails?) hair earth's grass
soul my breath and wind'

I said to (new-made) man
'what you can do
makes seven :
flesh hears
eye sees
soul scents

veins touch
blood tastes
you are boned
so be strong
find sweet joy
through mind'

this is the puzzle for him
in words I set that day :
'man held of what he does and does not see
lives and dies
figure him out'

*** little in his bigness
big in his littleness
speaks as well as
any I made ***

my second angel
of honor and glory

king of the world
sharing (Achamoth) my Wisdom

I made earth
his house
where none of all
I made who are
is his like

from the four hinges
(joining the lands' orb)
that also name
the four stars
I set for him
(*A*ntolia [rising/East]
  *D*ysis [setting/East]
  *A*rctos [the Bear/North]
  *M*esembria [mezzogiorno/South])
I called him Adam (Tetragrammaton)

I showed him
the two roads
of light and dark
'light is good
dark evil
I will find out
if you love
or hate me
if any of you
really do

what you do not
I know
who you are
you are ignorant of—so
you will go worse wrong
death follows sin'

I made him sleep
(his last word awake
was 'mother')
I took one of his ribs
and fleshed woman
for him to die through
I called her 'mother'
his last word 'Eve'

Paradise Park the sky opening the angels' victory song

Adam lived on earth
(where) I built (him) a garden
in the East in Eden
so he would obey my laws
and keep my word

I took the top off sky
he saw my angels
sing victory

Adam lived in the Garden
never leaving

the devil knew what I wanted
to make another world
because Adam ruled (this one)

devil : evil bottom agent

*** as a runaway he made
he made Sotona of sky ***

because he is called Satomaïl
he grew away from the angels
but what he is does not break his mind
he can still tell right from wrong
he knows why I threw him down
what he had done for me to do that

which is why he hated Adam
as thought he went between Eve's legs
without touching him

I curse ignorance
all I promised life
I do not turn from
and blight
I did not spoil man earth
or whatever else I did

I do damn his fruit
when it is rotten
when what he does
(brings on darkness)

rebel Adam driven out
God's desire not to destroy him
for all the years that will be

I said to him
'you are earth
back to the earth
I raised you from

I will not unmake you
but send you back
to the house of your birth
I promised life
to all I made
whether you see it or not'

Adam lived five and half hours
in Paradise

I blessed Sabbath
the seventh day
when people stop

the age of the world :

seven thousand years
the eighth thousandth ends
not years months weeks days

I drew up the eighth day
the first-made
after my creation

this is why
the first seven days (of the world)
return to figure
the first seven thousand years

when year eight thousand starts
time stops ending and rests
free from years months weeks days hours"

TWO STORIES FROM EZRA
THE APOCALYPTIST

A Latin text, c. third or fourth century A.D., from a Greek original, c. second century A.D. Text: Bensley, *The Fourth Book of Ezra*, in Robinson, ed., *Texts and Studies,* Vol. III.

1.

I said

Lord—if I have (ever) found grace before your eyes
reveal to your slave through whom you visit your creation

he said

the beginning of the Sphere of Earth
before the exits of time
before the conventicles of wind
before the voice of thunder
before the lightning flash
before elegant flowers
before strengthening the powers of going
before gathering uncounted troupes of Messengers
before lifting up the heights of air
before naming the measures of sky fixed above Earth
before reckoning the worth of the footstool of Zion
before numbering the present
before sweeping away the inventions
             of those who sin now
             and sealing those who keep
             the treasury of faith
I thought
I did
      and no one else

I said

        what will be the separation of time?
        when will be the end of that that was?
                the beginning of that that is to follow?

he said

        from Abraham to Abraham
        from him Jacob and Esau
        he held Jacob's hand
                he held Esau's foot
                from the beginning
        Esau ends today
        Jacob begins tomorrow
        . . . the hand of a man . . .
        between the heel and the hand
        look for nothing else
        Ezra

2.

I said

        Lord—speaking you told me of the beginning of creation
        you said "let sky and earth be done"

            and your word did

                wind flying
              shadow surrounding
                  silence

            man's voice not sounding in front of you
                      not yet

        you said "take a light from my light"
                take it from my treasuries
                to make my work seen

on the second day you made Wind of the sky fixed above Earth
you told him to divide
he divided Water
he made her go up in part
part he made stay below

on the third day you told Water to assemble
on 1/7 of Earth
you dried out 6/7 of Earth
saving her
to be planted and sown
to give you food and drink
out in the open

your word went out
the deed was done

there came
the fruit of endless abundance
in desire of taste in many forms
and flowers of colors we cannot do
and perfumes of scents we cannot find

on the fourth day you ordered sun's splendor moon's glow
stars spread out
you said
"wait on man"

on the fifth day you told the 1/7 where Water was assembled
to make the birds and fish

Water (who) had become silent and breathless
made them as you told her to
so that the peoples would talk of your wonderful deeds
you saved two
whom you called Behemoth and Leviathan
you separated them from each other

the 1/7 where Water was assembled could not hold them
you gave Behemoth the 1/7
which was dried out on the third day
to live where there are 1,000 hills

you gave Leviathan the 1/7 of Water

you saved them to feed those you want and when

on the sixth day you told Earth to make out in the open
the beasts of burden
the wild animals
and snakes

you made Adam lead everything you made

THE *SEFER YETZIRA*

The Book of Creation (Sefer Yetzira), a Hebrew text of the mystic tradition (Neo-Pythagorean), c. third–sixth centuries A.D. Text: The four texts in *Sefer Yetzira,* Lewin-Epstein Publishers, Jerusalem, 1965.

With 32 wondrous ways of wisdom

    YAH
    YHVH TSEVA'OT (OF HOSTS)
    ELOHEI YISRAEL (GOD OF ISRAEL)
    ELOHIM HAYIM (LIVING GOD)
    EL SHADAI (OMNIPOTENT GOD)
    RAM VE-NISA' (RAISED HIGH)
    SHOKHEN 'AD (ETERNAL DWELLER)

His Name high and holy

carved, covenanted, drilled, and created his world,

through three Sefarim:

    Sefer (book)=writing
    Sfor (counting)=number
    Sippur (telling)=speech

Ten Sefirot (numbers) made of Nothingness
Twenty-two Foundation Letters

Ten Sefirot as the number of the ten fingers
5 paralleling 5
    the Covenant set in the middle
the way the tongue makes the word   the Naked Word

Ten Sefirot of Nothingness Ten and not Nine Ten and not Eleven
    Understand this wisely Search it out intelligently

    Measure with them Search out from them

Know and consider   then Be Silent:

Set the Word at its Origin & return the Maker to His Place

For He is the Maker   creating alone   He has no peer
and Their number is Ten   and They have no end

Ten Sefirot made of Nothing
                    Brake your heart from thinking too quickly
                    Brake your mouth from speaking

                    If your heart races ahead
                    return
                    for it is said
                    "the creatures ran and returned"

                    The Covenant was made for this

Ten Sefirot made of Nothing
                    Their end is lodged in Their beginning
                    Their beginning in Their end
                    a flame and a coal

                    Know
                    then consider then Be silent:
                    that the Lord is unique
                    the Maker is one
                    He has no peer.

                    What number comes before One?

Ten Sefirot made of Nothing
                    Their number is Ten   and They have no end

                    The range of beginning
                    the range of end

                    The range of good
                    the range of evil

                    The range of height
                    the range of depth

The range of east
the range of west

The range of north
the range of south

Only Lord
God Faithful King
Patent of all
from the Residence of His Holiness to Eternity

Ten Sefirot made of Nothing
                    Their appearance is the look of lightning
                    Their disappearance: They have no end

                    His Word is in them as they come and go
                    At His command They race like the whirlwind
                    and bow before His throne

Ten Sefirot made of Nothing
Twenty-two Foundation Letters
Three Mothers
Seven Doubles
Twelve Simples

The Spiritwind in each of them

Ten Sefirot made of Nothing
                The first: The Spiritwind of Living God
            His throne set from the beginning
            Blessed the Name of Eternal Life   forever continually
            Voice   and Spiritwind   and Speech

            The Speech   the Holy Spiritwind
            Origin without beginning
            End beyond ending

Ten Sefirot made of Nothing
                    The first: The Spiritwind of Living God

                    The second: Wind from the Spiritwind

                    The third: Water from the Wind

                    The fourth: Fire from the Water
                              and height and depth
                              and East and West
                              and North and South

The second: Wind from the Spiritwind
                         He carved and lawed by them:
                    the four winds of the skies
                    East and West
                    North and South

                    The Spiritwind in each of them

The third: Water from Wind
                         He carved and lawed by them:
                    Tohu and Bohu
                    Mud and Clay

                    He made them a garden
                    Set them a wall
                    Roofed them with plaster
                    Poured snow upon them   and it became dust
                    as it is said:
                    "He said to the snow 'Be earth' "

                    Tohu a green line which surrounds the world
                    Bohu stones leveled and sunk in the Deep
                    water comes out from between them

The fourth: Fire from Water

He carved and lawed by it:
Glory Throne
Serafim
Ofanim
Creatures of Holy   they are the
Serving Angels

From the three of them He founded His place
as it is said:
"He makes His angels spiritwinds
                His servants a flaming fire"

The fifth: Sealed the height
                He chose three of the Simple letters
                fixed them by His Great Name YHV
                sealed by them the six directions:

He turned Up   Sealed it by HYV

The sixth: Sealed the under
                He turned Below   Sealed it by YVH

The seventh: Sealed east
                Turned before   Sealed it by VYH

The eighth: Sealed west
                Turned behind   Sealed it by VHY

The ninth: Sealed south
                Turned right   Sealed it by YHV

The tenth: Sealed north
                Turned left   Sealed it by HVY

These are the ten Sefirot made of Nothing:

The first: The Spiritwind of Living God

The second: Wind from the Spiritwind

The third: Water from the Wind

The fourth: Fire from the Water

and height
and depth
and East
and West
and North
and South

Twenty-two Foundation Letters
Three Mothers
Seven Doubles
Twelve Simples

All of   them are Lawed by the voice
                    Carved by the breathwind
                    Fixed by the mouth at five places

ALEF   ḤET   HE   'AYIN

GIMEL YOD   KAF   KUF

DALET   TET   LAMED   NUN   TAV

ZAYIN   SAMEKH   TZADI   RESH   SHIN

BET   VAV   MEM   PE

as much a part of the tongue they are as a flame and a coal

ALEF   ḤET   HE   'AYIN   made where the end of the tongue
                                           comes against the throat

BET   VAV   MEM   PE   between the lips
                                        at the head of the tongue

GIMEL YOD   KAF   KUF   on the back third
                                        of a divided tongue

DALET TET LAMED NUN TAV   the head of the tongue
made by the voice

ZAYIN SAMEKH TZADI RESH SHIN   between the teeth
the tongue low and flat

Twenty-two Foundation Letters
fixed on the wheel at 231 Gates
the wheel turns forward and back

The mark of a thing/word:
if good   nothing is greater than happiness
if evil   nothing is worse than torture

Twenty-two letters He:

           Lawed
           Carved
           Weighed
           Combined

                ALEF with all of them
           Combined them and made
           the soul of all made things
           and the soul of all things to be made

How did He weigh them and combine them?

           ALEF with all of them
           all with ALEF

           BET with all of them
           all with BET

           and so with all of them
           returning empty
           going out from the 231 Gates
           so that all the souls of all made things
           and all speech
           comes out of one Name

He made the Distinct from the Indistinct
   made the Nothing Something
   carved great rocks from the air that has no substance

The three Mothers   ALEF   MEM   SHIN
are like a scales   one plate for what is earned
      one for what is owed

      the tongue of law keeps them apart

The three Mothers ALEF   MEM   SHIN
are a great secret
covered   wondrous   hidden   by six rings
Fire   Water and Wind come out of them
dividing into male and female

Know   Consider   and Be Silent
Fire bears Water

The three Mothers   ALEF   MEM   SHIN
the birth of the sky is from fire
the birth of the air is from wind
the birth of the earth is from water

Fire above   water beneath
the tongue of law keeps them apart

From them Fathers were born
and from them All was made

The three Mothers   ALEF   MEM   SHIN
are   in the world   Wind   Water   and Fire
   the sky made from Fire
   the earth from Water
   the air from Wind keeps them apart

The three Mothers   ALEF   MEM   SHIN
are   in the year   heat   cold   and wet

```
heat    made from Fire
cold    made from Water
wet     made from Wind    keeps them apart
```

The three Mothers   ALEF   MEM   SHIN
are   in the being head   belly   and organ
     the head made from Fire
     the belly made from Water
     the organ made from Wind keeping them apart

The three Mothers   ALEF   MEM   SHIN
He lawed them
   carved them
   combined them
   sealed by them

The three Mothers   ALEF   MEM   SHIN
are   in the world

The three Mothers   ALEF   MEM   SHIN
are   in the year

The three Mothers   ALEF   MEM   SHIN
are   in the being   male and female

He made the letter ALEF king in the air   crowned it   (=*'avir*)
   combined the letters one with another
   made by it:
        air   in the world
        wet   in the year
        organ   in the living being   male and female

He made the letter MEM king in the water   (=*mayim*)
   crowned it
   combined the letters one with another
   made by it:

```
earth   in the world
cold    in the year
belly   in the living being    male and female
```

He made the letter SHIN king in fire   (=*'esh*)
   crowned it
   combined the letters one with another
   made by it:

```
            sky     in the world
            heat    in the year
            head    in the living being   male and female
```

How did He combine them?

```
            ALEF  MEM   SHIN
            ALEF  SHIN  MEM
            MEM   ALEF  SHIN
            MEM   SHIN  ALEF
            SHIN  ALEF  MEM
            SHIN  MEM   ALEF
```

```
Sky=Fire          Man's head=Fire
Air=Wind          Man's belly=Water
Earth=Water       Man's heart=Wind
```

The three Mothers ALEF   MEM   SHIN

                                      made with

ALEF Wind   Air   Wet   Organ   lawed Tongue between

                                      made with

MEM   Water   Earth   Cold   Belly   plate for what is owned

                                      made with

SHIN   Fire   Sky   Heat   Head   plate for what is owed

             These are ALEF   MEM   SHIN

The seven Doubles BET GIMEL DALET KAF PE RESH TAV

Founded in Life Peace Wisdom and Richness and Progeny
       and Favor and Governance

                                                   behave
in double utterance realized in double:

    BET/VET GGIMEL/GIMEL DDALET/DALET
    KAF/KHAF PE/FE RRESH/RESH TTAV/TAV
a soft and a hard form a hero and a weakling

These are the doubles:
                  Wisdom/Folly   Richness/Poverty
                  Progeny/Barrenness   Life/Death
                  Governance/Slavery   Peace/War
                  Favor/Ugliness

The seven Doubles BET GIMEL DALET KAF PE RESH TAV
Seven and not six
Seven and not eight
Six sides and six chambers of the Temple
the Holy Palace set in the middle

        Blessed the Glory of God in His Place
        He is the Place of the world
        The world is not his Place
        He bears it all

Seven Doubles BET GIMEL DALET KAF PE RESH TAV
                of Foundation

He lawed them
He carved them
He combined them
He weighed them
He exchanged them
He made by them: the seven stars of the world
                        the seven days of the year
                        the seven gates of the soul

                        seven and seven

How did he join them?

> Two stones building two houses
> Three stones building six houses
> Four stones building twenty-four houses
> Five stones
> building one hundred and twenty houses
> Six stones
> building seven hundred and twenty houses
> Seven stones
> building five thousand and forty houses

> from this point on you must go
>   and think upon
> what the mouth cannot say
> and   the ear cannot hear

He made the letter BET king in Wisdom
   crowned it
   combined it with the others
   made from it:
>   Saturn   in the world
>   Sabbath   in the year
>   Mouth   in the being
>   male and female

He made the letter GIMEL king in Richness
   crowned it
   combined it with the others
   made from it:
>   Jupiter   in the world
>   Sunday   in the year
>   The Right Eye   in the being
>   male and female

He made the letter DALET king in Progeny
   crowned it
   combined it with the others
   made from it:

                    Mars   in the world
                    Monday   in the year
                    The Left Eye   in the being
                                        male and female

He made the letter KAF king in Life
    crowned it
    combined it with the others
    made from it:
                        Sun   in the world
                        Tuesday   in the year
                        The Right Nostril   in the being
                                        male and female

He made the letter PE king in Governance
    crowned it
    combined it with the others
    made from it:
                            Venus   in the world
                            Wednesday   in the year
                            The Left Nostril   in the being
                                        male and female

He made the letter RESH king in Peace
    crowned it
    combined it with the other letters
    made from it:
                            Mercury   in the world
                            Thursday   in the year
                            The Right Ear   in the being
                                        male and female

He made the letter TAV king in Favor
    crowned it
    combined it with the other letters
    made from it:

Moon   in the world
Friday   in the year
The Left Ear   in the being
           male and female

By them he carved out:
       Seven Heavens
       Seven Earths
       Seven Seas
       Seven Rivers
       Seven Deserts
       Seven Days
       Seven Weeks
       Seven Years
       Seven Sabbatical Years
       Seven Jubilees

       The Holy Palace therefore he carved
as the seventh of every desire beneath the skies

Seven stars in the world:
       Saturn
       Jupiter
       Mars
       Sun
       Venus
       Mercury
       Moon

Seven days in the year:
       The seven days of the week

Seven gates in the being   male and female:

Two eyes
Two ears
Two nostrils
the mouth

Seven Heavens:

Vilon	(Curtain)
Raki'a'	(Divider)
Sheḥakim	(Clouded Heaven)
Zevul	(Dwelling)
Ma'on	(Habitation)
Makhon	(Establishment)
'Aravot	(Hidden Clouds)

Seven earths:

'Adama	(Manearth)
Tevel	(Vegetative earth)
Neshiya	(Underworld)
Tziya	(Desert earth)
Ḥeled	(Dust earth)
'Eretz	(Earth)
Gai'	(Valley)

Each one He made unto itself:

The world to itself
The being to itself
The year to itself

Seven Doubles BET GIMEL DALET KAF PE RESH TAV

made by
BET: Saturn Sabbath and Mouth Life Death

made by
GIMEL: Jupiter Sunday Right Eye Peace Evil

made by
DALET: Mars Monday Left Eye Wisdom Folly

                                                              made by
KAF: Sun   Tuesday   Right Nostril   Richness   Poverty

                                                              made by
PE: Venus   Wednesday   Left Nostril   Progeny   Barrenness

                                                              made by
RESH: Mercury   Thursday   Right Ear   Favor   Ugliness

                                                              made by
TAV: Moon   Friday   Left Ear   Governance   Slavery

     These are BET   GIMEL   DALET   KAF   PE   RESH   TAV

Twelve Simples: HE VAV ZAYIN ḤET TET YOD LAMED
                 NUN SAMEKH 'AYIN TZADI KUF

Their Foundation: Twelve   not eleven   Twelve   not thirteen

Twelve
Their Foundation: Seeing   Hearing   Smelling   Talking   Tasting
                  Sexual intercourse   Movement   Anger   Laughter
                  Thought   Doing   Sleep

Twelve slant directions divided into six groups
                    separating wind from wind:

   The Up-East line   The North-East line   The Down-East line
   The Up-South line   The South-East line   The Down-South line
   The Up-West line   The South-West line   The Down-West line
   The Up-North line   The North-East line   The Down-North line

Spreading   Spreading   to Eternity forever
They are the very arms of the world

Twelve Simples: HE VAV ZAYIN ḤET TET YOD LAMED
                 NUN SAMEKH 'AYIN TZADI KUF

He lawed them
   carved them
   combined them
   weighed them
   exchanged them
   made by them:

           The Twelve Constellations   in the world
           The Twelve Months   in the year
           The Twelve Media   in the being
                                        male and female

two of them Joying   two of them Slandering
two of them Instructive   two of them Rejoicing
two of them Tearing   two of them Chasing

the stomach and the spleen   the gall and the liver
the kidneys   the gullet and the anus
the hands   the feet
                              He set them up as a sort of
battle line   one across from the other:

They stand in groups of Three:
                         Each one by itself
                         One accusing
                         One defending
                         One separating these two

They stand in groups of Seven:
                         Three against Three
                         One separating these two

Twelve in battle order:
                         Three loving
                         Three warring
                         Three giving life
                         Three killing

Three loving:
                         Heart
                         Ears
                         Eyes

Three hating:
                         Liver
                         Gall
                         Tongue

Three giving life:

> Nostril
> Nostril
> Spleen

Three killing:

> Gullet
> Anus
> Mouth

> God Faithful King governs all of them
> from His Place of Glory to the End of Eternity

One on three
Three on seven
Seven on Twelve
all devoted to each other: A proof of the matter:

> Twenty-two desires   One body

How did he join them?

He made the letter HE king in Speech
   crowned it
   combined it with the others
   made by it:

Aries	in the world
Nisan	in the year
Liver	in the being male and female

He made the letter VAV king in Thought
   crowned it
   combined it with the others
   made by it:

Taurus	in the world
'Iyar	in the year
Spleen	in the being male and female

He made the letter ZAYIN king in Movement
    crowned it
    combined it with the others
    made by it:

Gemini	in the world	
Sivan	in the year	
Gall	in the being	male and female

He made the letter ḤET king in Seeing
    crowned it
    combined it with the others
    made by it:

Cancer	in the world	
Tamuz	in the year	
Stomach	in the being	male and female

He made the letter TET king in Hearing
    crowned it
    combined it with the others
    made by it:

Leo	in the world	
'Av	in the year	
Right Kidney	in the being	male and female

He made the letter YOD king in Doing
    crowned it
    combined it with the others
    made by it:

Virgo	in the world	
'Elul	in the year	
Left Kidney	in the being	male and female

He made the letter LAMED king in Sexual Intercourse
    crowned it
    combined it with the others
    made by it:

Libra	in the world	
Tishrei	in the year	
Anus	in the being	male and female

He made the letter NUN king in Smelling
    crowned it
    combined it with the others
    made by it:

Scorpio	in the world	
Marḥeshvan	in the year	
Gullet	in the being	male and female

He made the letter SAMEKH king in Sleep
    crowned it
    combined it with the others
    made by it:

Sagittarius	in the world	
Kislev	in the year	
Right Hand	in the being	male and female

He made the letter 'AYIN king in Anger
    crowned it
    combined it with the others
    made by it:

Capricorn	in the world	
Tevet	in the year	
Left Hand	in the being	male and female

He made the letter TZADI king in Taste
    crowned it
    combined it with the others
    made by it:

Aquarius	in the world	
Shevat	in the year	
Right Leg	in the being	male and female

He made the letter KUF king in Laughter
   crowned it
   combined it with the others
   made by it:

Pisces	in the world	
'Adar	in the year	
Left Leg	in the being	male and female

He divided them into groups   set them apart   each to itself
the world   to itself   the year   to itself
                  the being   to itself   male and female

Twelve Simples: HE VAV ZAYIN ḤET TET YOD LAMED
                 NUN SAMEKH 'AYIN TZADI KUF

                                                    made by
HE   Aries   Nisan   Liver   Seeing   Blindness

                                                    made by
VAV   Taurus   'Iyar   Spleen   Hearing   Deafness

                                                    made by
ZAYIN   Gemini   Sivan   Gall   Smelling   Anosmia

                                                    made by
ḤET   Cancer   Tamuz   Stomach   Speaking   Dumbness

                                                    made by
TET   Leo   'Av   Right Kidney   Tasting   Hunger

                                                    made by
YOD   Virgo   'Elul   Left Kidney   Doing   Handicap

                                                    made by
LAMED   Libra   Tishrei   Anus   Coition   Impotence

                                                    made by
NUN   Scorpio   Marḥeshvan   Gullet   Movement   Lameness

					made by
SAMEKH	Sagittarius	Kislev	Right Hand	Anger	Liver ailment

					made by
'AYIN	Capricorn	Tevet	Left Hand	Laughter	Gall ailment

					made by
TZADI	Aquarius	Shevat	Right Leg	Thought	Heart ailment

					made by
KUF	Pisces	'Adar	Left Leg	Sleep	Waking

These are the Simples

HE   VAV   ZAYIN   ḤET   TET   YOD   LAMED
NUN   SAMEKH   'AYIN   TZADI   KUF

All of them sharing   as in a quiver   or a wheel   or the heart

Three Mothers   ALEF   MEM   SHIN
Seven Doubles   BET   GIMEL   DALET   KAF   PE   RESH   TAV
Twelve Simples   HE   VAV   ZAYIN   ḤET   TET   YOD   LAMED
NUN   SAMEKH   'AYIN   TZADI   KUF

Three fathers and their progeny   Seven planets and their attendants
Twelve slant directions

Every desire   one against another   God made:
Good   over against   Bad   Bad over against Good
Good   from Good   Bad   from   Bad
Good   makes Bad distinct   Bad   makes Good distinct
Good   kept for the goodly   Bad   kept for the evil

. . .

Part Two

Elemental Creation

I. RISING

A RITUAL FOR THE PURIFICATION
OF A TEMPLE

A Sumero-Akkadian text, this is an important bridge piece connecting these diverse peoples (cp. relevant passages in the Sumerian *Enki and Ninhursag* and *The Deluge* with the Akkadian *Enuma eliš*). Text: F. Thureau-Dangin, *Rituels accadiens.*

Bright house   god house   holy place   not yet
no reed up   no tree made
no brick down   no house up
no house up   no city set
no city set   no being being

no Nippur set   no Ekur built
no Uruk made   no Eana built

no Apsu-house built   no Eridu built

no place   for the bright house   the god house   made

no land   sea

motion in sea cunt

Eridu made   Ešagil rising
Lugaldukuda stays   in Ešagil   in sea cunt
Babylon city built   Ešagil complete

Marduk made pure city   heart's love
for the Igigi   highest   they call it

Marduk sets reed on water
shapes dust   pours around reed
shapes man   for god rest   in house of heart's love

goddess Aruru makes man seed   with him
he shapes animals   and other life of field

he makes Tigris and Euphrates   sets them in their place
he calls their name in fortune
he makes grass   swamp weed   reed   forest
wild green plant   land   bog   swamp
wild cow   calf   ewe   and lamb domesticate
tree-gardens   forests
ram   and mountain goat

Bel Marduk   builds a dam   for the sea
shapes reeds   makes trees
sets bricks   raises buildings
makes houses   builds cities
beings being he made   in cities he made
he makes Nippur   builds Ekur
    makes Uruk   builds Eana

FROM THE PAPYRUS BREMNER-RHIND

This creation text from the Papyrus Bremner-Rhind contains
material dating back to c. 2300 B.C. Text: Wallis-Budge,
The Gods of the Egyptians.

the book of finding out the turnings of ⎰RA
                                  ⎱sun disc lord
and overthrowing ⎰APOPHIS
                      ⎱water snake

say these words
Ra said
after he was ⎰KHEPERA
                   ⎱beetle life maker

:

"I am who was Khepera
in the body of Khepera/dung beetle rolling the shitball sun
I turned Khepera
whowhich made everything that came into me

after I became Khepera
many others did too
walking out of my mouth

there was no beetle sky lady Nut
no beetle earth
no earth things lifting off the land
or animals creeping there

I lifted them up/right armhand doing it
out of ⎰NUN
       ⎱the layered waters of the deep
where they were not busy
where my feet could not stand

so I charmed my heart to advantage
built the platform of the world in ⎧MAA
⎩truth straightness

I gave each characteristics
my right eye seeing/doing

I was all alone
⎧SHU   not spat from my mouth
⎩daddy airs
or ⎧TEFNUT   like barley from the earth
    ⎩ma waters

no one else lived in beetle
whose right eye saw/did with mine

I made a platform in my heart talking it into act
there came
the many living things
that came into beetle
children into beetle life
and their children
from birth
from the living things came into beetle
from their births
from their children's children's beetle bodies

yes I
it was me
grabbed my cock
drained seedwater
through my fist back into me
I wrapped myself around cock
joined   in fucking my shadow
fanning me under his cloud
I rained seedwater
spewing it like barley from the earth
into my mouth my own

I sprouted back windman Shu
I dropped raingirl Tefnut

84   ORIGINS

my father ⌠NUN   cared for them
    ⌡sky water deep
my right eye which sees/does
right behind them
from the time they walked from me

after I turned beetle god one and lonely god
three came out of my mouth into Khepera
also gods but later than I in this earth
while Shu and Tefnut
raised up out of limp water
found their happiness in Nun

in their following
they brought me
my busy right eye
I tied it to all of my flesh parts back to my heart
and wept [*remit*] over them
that's how people [*romet*] came to life in Khepera
men and women
from the tears pouring from the box of my true right eye

who was angry taking a stick against me
after he'd walked up and found
I'd made another
a false one
to take his place
I gave him fame gave him splendid acts
glories I'd made for myself

so he had to resume his way in the right socket of my face
later to rule this earth far as it is wide
his anger fell away
I gave him what had been lost

I raced up through the plant roots
through everything that snakes along
into all who live in Khepera

god lords Shu and Tefnut
had the children ⎧GEB   and ⎧NUT
                  ⎩Earth   ⎩Sky

god lords Geb and Nut
had the children
Osiris
Horus Khenti-en-irti
Seth
Isis
Nephthys
from the body of their womb
one after the other
they did so
they split themselves into children
in this earth"

FROM THE EGYPTIAN *BOOK OF THE DEAD*

A creation text from the Egyptian *Book of the Dead,* c. 2000–
1500 B.C. Text: Wallis-Budge, *The Egyptian Book of the Dead.*
"/. . ./" denotes explanations; "(. . .)" denotes hieroglyphs.

I am   (bowl   lord all   fluid   owl) ATUM   completing-rising
               of all
the only one
in Nun /chaos-fluid/

I am RA
  (sitting hawk-head   resting   cobra-cock circling SunDisk)
  in first (lotus   papyrus acres   starting up   Horushawk   handgiving)
      I ruled this
he did

Who is he?
Is RA
      in first
        when he rose (sun bursting over landline   two arms giving)
       in Shu /town/ (as king sat   spoke sealines and ground apart)

      before the pillars (more than three   under NUT /sky woman/)
           of Shu were
when RA was
           upon
the high land of
                Khemennu /Hermopolis–Thothtown/ (eight gods)

I am
the god
the great
who lived
into life by myself (snakebody)
                NUN
who lifted clear   speaking
           his own name:

"Paut neteru" /company of nine gods/
as god

Who is he then?

He is RA   naming   his flesh pieces
are   young   alive

as gods who are the standing feet of RA

I am
without anything giving repulse
in gods

Who is he then?
ATUM he is
in his SunDisk
RA
in rising   going out
in the eastern line of heaven

I am
yesterday
know
tomorrow

Who is he then?

Yesterday OSIRIS (a throne above the Horuseye   a seated god)
Tomorrow
the day his enemies
enemies of NEBERTCHER
    (all lord   open mouth   bound offering   seated god) /OSIRIS/
are destroyed
RA
choosing as ruler
his son HORUS (Horushawk   seated god)
or
some say
the day we set up
the holiday
of meeting: the corpse which is OSIRIS

                    and
          his father
during the making
of battle
by the gods
when the commander giving orders
was OSIRIS   Lord Amentet

What is it then?
Amentet (the world   under earth   out West)

the making of the souls
            (bowl of burning incense   bearded Horushawk)
of the gods
when the commander commanding was OSIRIS
in Set-Amentet
   (mountain/desert land and   the world   under earth   out West)
Set-Amentet   others call
Amentet
is
that which is
which makes
RA
stand and fight for it
when a god
any god
comes into it

I know the god
that god is in it.

Who is he then?

OSIRIS he is
others call RA
his name
the cock   (horizontal cock raining seedwater)
is RA's
when he fucks in strength
with
himself

I am
bennubird /the phoenix/
that bennubird which is
in Heliopolis /SunTown/

I am the doer executing
the book
of those madelings   alive now
and later

Who is he then?

He is OSIRIS
others say:
his own corpse is he
other people say
his shitting and pissing
!!!
those creations alive
now and later
make his corpse
others say
!!!

Eternity   (rooster   looping ropewick   SunDisk)
he is and
he lasts forever

Eternity is the day
!!!
He-lasts-forever is
Night
!!!
I am AMSU   (Standard)
in his seeming   (coming out)
his feathers on my head

Who is this then?
AMSU is HORUS
father's avenger
born coming out of godhouse

FRAGMENTS FROM MOUSAIOS

From Mousaios, the reputed son and secretary of Orpheus, a Greek text traditionally dated c. 1000 B.C., drawn from contemporaneous Phoenician and Egyptian sources. Text: Diels-Kranz, *Die Fragmente der Vorsokratiker,* Vol. 1. Numbers according to Diels-Kranz.

3. the eagle lays three eggs, two he hatches, one he leaves

5. but the fields give life to the leaves
   some die on the ash trees
   others live on

   our life those leaves

8.   The Story of Zeus Goat Skin Wearer

When Zeus was born
Rhea gave him to Themis
Themis gave him to Amalthea
but she gave him to Goat
Goat, daughter of the Sun
raised him in a cave on Crete
where his father, Kronos
couldn't find him

she fed him her milk

he grew up
he fought the Titans

since he didn't have any weapons
the oracle told him
"use Goat's skin for your shield
it can't be hurt, besides
Gorgon's head is in the middle"
that's what he did
and the skin stretched twice as large

Goat's bones he wrapped in another skin
gave them life, then life beyond death
set her up there among the stars

that's why we call Zeus "Goat Skin Wearer"

11. She-earth spoke an understanding word
    Fiery, famous Earth-Shaker's helper, agreed

14. Pit was first and Night
    the first goddess

16. Comets fall up from Ocean
    into Sky where they are born

THE ORPHIC COSMOGONY
ACCORDING TO EUDEMOS

The "usual" Orphic cosmology according to Eudemos. A Greek text from the fourth century B.C. from Greek sources, c. 700–600 B.C. Text: a combination of two fragments, one from Damascius, *De Principiis,* the other from a critic of the second or third century A.D., Achilles Statius of Byzantium, both in Diels-Kranz, *Die Fragmente der Vorsokratiker,* Vol. 1.

Chronos

then FireAir   Gap

for everything that is

Egg

(this is the first three)

the second three

brooding

Egg is seeded as 1. God
                    2. WhiteBright Robe
                    3. Cloud

from the second three Phanes

the third three

1. Metis who is mind
2. Erikepaios who is power
3. Phanes who is father

but what happened to Egg?

shell is sky
membrane FireAir

THE ORPHIC COSMOGONY
ACCORDING TO ATHENAGORAS

A Greek text from the fourth century A.D. from older Greco-Roman Orphic sources, probably dating back to the time of *Sacred Stories* (sixth century B.C.). Text: Kern, *Orphicorum Fragmenta.*

Water

       from him Mud

             they had a child
                the dragon snaked
                   lion-headed
                god-faced between
           Chronos/Heracles

      Heracles laid a giant egg

        so filled by father Chronos

            it split

       the top sky Ouranos
       the bottom earth Gea

         and a god double-bodied . . . [Phanes?]

Ouranos slept with Gea
     girls:
       Klotho
       Lachesis
       Atropos
     boys:
       The Hundred-handed: Kottos Gyges Briareus
       The Cyclops: Brontes Steropes Arges

FROM PHERECYDES OF SYROS,

THE SEVEN NOOKS

Fragments from *The Seven Nooks* of Pherecydes of Syros. A Greek text from the early seventh century B.C. Text: Diels-Kranz, *Die Fragmente der Vorsokratiker,* Vol. 1, except for 1a. which is in Damascius, *De Principiis* (Ruelle, ed.). Numbers heading sections correspond to the numbered fragments in Diels-Kranz.

1.

Z—Day   Time   She-earth
the always living

She-earth became our earth
Z—Day gave her earth for her honorable share

1a.

Chronos took his come
and slapped together
        wind   fire   water
        who split into 5 nooks
        wombs of the other gods

           FiveNook

      making   FiveWorld[s]

2.

    The Story of the Flying Tree of Earth
    (on which She hung the web of cloth)

they are building houses for Z—Day
many houses huge houses
they put everything he'll need into them
they give men and women to serve him
and anything else he might need

when everything is ready
they have the wedding

on the third day of the wedding
Z—Day makes a web of cloth
a large and lovely mantle
he embroiders Earth and Ocean on it
and the houses of Ocean

[he gives it to his bride She-earth
he says to her]
"because you wish to marry
I give you this for honorable share
take pleasure in me
join me in love"

people say
this was the first rite of the unveiling
this is how the custom arose
among gods and men

after she receives the web of cloth
she says to him

3.

when he was about to make the world
Z—Day changed into Eros

he made the world out of contradictions
he drove agreement and love through it
he extended it into one throughout

4.

Kronos and Snake went to war
they raised up armies
they challenged each other and fought
then they made an agreement
whoever fell into Ocean first lost
the winner to be Sky-master

this is the beginning
of the mysteries of the Titans and Geagants
who people say fought the gods

and the stories   the Egyptians tell
of ⎰TYPHOON and Horus and Osiris
  ⎱Seth

5.

below our part of the world
is the share of Tartaros the Terrible

Snatchers and Hurricane
Northwind's daughters
stand guard there

whoever injures him
Zeus throws Tartaros

6.

hollows, ditches, caves, gates
riddles through which
souls pass and repass
this men call birth and death

the ordered world is a cave

7.

seed pours out

12.

the gods call a table *thyoros*
because that's where people
put out food for them

13.

Zeus and Hera are not the parents of the gods

13a.

gods eat immortality

FROM THE *SACRED STORIES*
OF ONOMACRITOS (?)

This Greek text was also known as the *Rhapsodic Theogony,* possibly compiled by Onomacritos, an early editor of Homer, c. 550 B.C. It was taken from Greco-Phoenician sources after 1100 B.C. and formed the Orphics' major sacred book. A full listing of the fragments is found at the end of this selection. "[. . .]" denotes material added for narrative continuity. ". . ." denotes material omitted. "***" denotes gaps in the original Greek text. "'. . .'" denotes verses cited by the ancients as stemming directly from Orpheus himself c. 1000 B.C. "⟨. . .⟩" denotes words which may be disregarded.

1.

[I, Orpheus, said]

' King Apollo
      Leto's son
   shooting from afar
         Phoibos of power '

       Lord   day son who hits everything
           with the arrows of your ray

         even though   far away
     unsullied can do-er ' see-all
lording dier and deathless alike '

         who sees everyone
     king of gods and men

' Sun rising on golden wing '
    Helios in air   on precious wing

‘ I heard the 12th voice come from you ’
I listened to the god voice
in twelves
[or: twelve times]

‘ when you came in brightness   shooter from afar
divine testifier ’
when you spoke to me
I witnessed you shining in the farness
[tell me
how   it all began]

2.
[& Apollo told me:]
START
⟨workman in⟩ Chronos/'Olam
makes FireAir
that Chaos/Egg a belt rings
yes dark cloud
gripping in her domes
everything under FireAir

but   before   above   inside
PHANES   who made them
whom you can't touch   can't hold
fathermother of Night   FireAir
and all the diacosm

[slept] in gloom in Chaos/Egg
wrapped in FireAir

Earth   unseen shadowy

Light/Phanes
shattering FireAir
piercing Chaos
blinding Earth and everything else
Phanes—Metis—Erikepaios [the three in one] who mean
'Light Giver of Life'
from himher
bodiless beginnings

                                        & sun   moon   means   stars
                  earth   sea   the world   seen and unseen

3.

[They tell it another way]

            Chronos/'Olam   ▽   Rhea [Lady Hyle]
                      Egg

                               remember?

Egg   in Chronos   in time
                spinning   warming
                        makes SkyHeaven
                              who is round   half
                                  & screwed on top of Earth

Egg filled to bursting
                  one chrome
                        one skin   & color
                          his body: phantasy
                  think of a peacock's egg
                            inside
                            the 1,000 colors of its fan
                      so Egg grew
                          stocked with the Wind
                              that blows out
                              the endless colors
                                  of everything
                                that breathes

Egg   like a top
                turning in the currents of Lady Hyle
                    see there every change light brings

inside:
    the godwind racing up and down
        the malefemale
           doing it by thought
    Phanes [Metis Erikepaios]
        bright Phancy
the torch
    firing the diacosm
'telesphoros'
        [beginning   ending
        year accomplisher
        to fulfill purpose
        ordering managing favoring]
          lightning bug
          lamp in the water

yes   warm   hot   ripe   Egg
    broke on the inside
        ' when the [clay?] gaping egg
           yawns: cracks: '
        Phanes
          steps out
             to make the world
             a harmony
             that coheres

4.

for Phanes
        authors all the gods
          built them a sky
            & for their children
    ' for those who do not die
        he made a home that does not wear out '

31.

        seeded the Golden Race [in Metis]

5.

      and was the   first king of the gods

6.

he/she has a number: 12

        from the completed number of the 3rd
        & of the 4th that brings to birth—
            worker in 'mixing and mingling'
            cupping the bright diacosm of the gods

$$3 \quad \times \quad 4 \quad = 12$$

starts
 1
 &
 2
 of
 3
 &
 4

 1 = FireAir   (+ 1)
 2 = Gap/Chaos(+ 1)
 3 = Egg   who is completed   (by +1)
─
 4 = *Phanes*
      # ' seen to 4 eyes everythere '

    Erikepaios

5.

    Metis

       ' fearful angel '
       carrying glorious godsperm
       whom the Blessed on Olympos
       call
           ' Phanes FirstBorn '

3.

    then Phanes goes away
           sits in one of the crags of skyheaven
             [in the cave of Daughter Night]
           where in secret ways
               he lights up
           [the comings and goings   of]
           boundless time

9.

      don't ask questions
        give up

           Phanes and Night rule skyheaven

31.

            she the second queen
           holding the scepter
             he/she made

9.

. . .

seated in the nook of her cave
        they last out time
           in the inmost unseen cryptic adytos
           Phanes
             and Daughter Night
          who gives the gods
          oracles
          [that never fail]

     call them
      and you wouldn't be wrong
        malefemale
      fathermother
         sunmoon   set among the Wanderers
         theone   that equals everyone

[* * *]

> the krater
>> mixing bowl
>>> where cupped
>>> in their embrace
>>> everysoul   sees life

8.

> *Iynges*
>> [wrynecks
>>> birds of magic

>> four spoked wheels

>>> (the malefemale)
>> Pothos (Hipeḥ) Eros]

7.

[Adrasteia serves them]
> alone the goddess of those who remain in Night
>> Melissos' and Amaltheia's daughter
> from their unswerving forethought
>>> ' pretty girl Ida and sperm sister Adrasteia '
>>> who takes   who holds within her
>> the measure of all practice in the diacosm
>>> inside and out

>>>> outside their Cave
> she whacks the   ' big bronze kettledrums Night gave her '
>>> by the door
>>> pounding drum tambourine cymbal
>>> so all can hear her laws

11.

' [beneath the stars that] see white

[that] glitterflash in the dusky cloth of Night '

8.

' Phanes broke the virgin flower
of Daughter [Night] '

10.

children:
Skyheaven/Uranos
Earth/Ge
The Cyclops
The Hundred Handed
Skyheaven was their first child
he shone
because his father was god of light

8.

he fucked his sister [Ge]
just like   Daddy did [Night] Daughter

12.

the children

31.

whom Ge hid from their father the 3rd king Skyheaven

12.

        seven girls lovely and pure
          who roll their eyes in come hithers

                Themis
                wise Tethys
                Mnemosyné whose hair hangs down
                happy Theia
                Dioné—especially pretty
                Phoibé
                Rhea mother of king Zeus

        seven boys   wooly haired kings

                Koios
                big Krios
                strong Phorkys
                Kronos
                Ocean
                Hyperion
                Iapetos

14. [This is what Ocean and Kronos did]

Ocean   flows   backward   he hurries on himself
      it is better to say:
           he returns
              leading himself in circles
           around his mother Earth
              whom he holds inside himself
    ‘ the circle of lovely untiring rippling Ocean:
              rows around Earth
        keeping her all inside his swirls ’

31. & 16.

      [But Kronos rebelled]
          caught his dad
              cut off his balls
          became the 4th king
           maker of the Silver Race

28.

he was   'first to think around corners'
made everything return
to itself

13.

Mixer Kronos
hair on his chin always black
meaning that people then
refused   old age
and were always young

15.

[Kronos fucked his sister Rhea

children:
the Olympians
especially Zeus

Kronos swallowed them all: except Zeus
Rhea gave him a stone instead
sent Zeus to Crete
to Dicté's Cave
where Amaltheia Nursed him
& the Kouretes
beating their
shields
distracted daddy

when he grew up
he got his revenge
just like his father before him]

16.

                    caught him with honey
                              filled up Kronos with beer
                                                  drunk
                                        he passed out
        Night had told him

                    ' if you see your father under tall oaks
                       drunk with deeds of raspy buzzing bees
                       tie '   him   ' up '

                              tied him up   cut off his balls
                                        ' cutting and being cut '
                              o
                                  fathers and sons

17.

              the balls hit water and floated
                  all around
                              white foam spun
              in Hours' circles
                              Eniautos built inside (this spermy egg)
                              the modest Lady of Generation:

                  [Aphrodite]
                  who in her palms
                              as she was being born
                      took the first of jealousy and deceit

31.

18.

5th King Zeus
              before making anything
                              went to the oracles of Night
                              who filled him with thought
                              beginning things

and released his doubt:

     'father be the mother'

Zeus said:

    ' Eternal Night
             highest god   *maia*/nurse
                            how
                  tell me
                          how am I
                 strong heart
          to make
            the beginnings
            of gods?

19.

        how shall I be and have one and all
            and each thing separately? '

[Oracle Night:]

    ' swallow everything that nameless FireAir [Phanes is]
      in his/her body
        skyheaven
        immense earth
        sea
        & all stars that make the pictures
         skyheaven locks in circles

20.

      stretch a chain
        golden links of FireAir
    to bind [the diacosm Phanes the 1st World] '

21.

[so] Phanes First Born
        loveliest of those minded
                powered
                  & alive of self
       loneliest justicier of hisher making

Zeus swallowed
      on advice of Night

     ' Phanes Erikepaios held
             the body of everything
       in his hollow belly
         mixed in hisher bones & flesh
         the godpower
so that with himher [inside] everything could be made
      of Zeus
      once anew '

22.

     ' so with himher [inside]
       [The 2nd World] was made of Zeus once anew
         height of skyheaven and fireair
         couch of barren sea
            & glorious earth
      huge Ocean   Earth's deepest Tartara
         rivers
       sea more than enough
      and everything else
        including:
      all the gods and goddesses
        deathless and happy

   whatever was will be one is born
   mixing and mingling in Zeus's belly '

20.

      and he laid down a golden chain
                      [binding sky and earth]
        as Night told him

24.

But Phanes will return

31.

    he is Dionysos the 6th king

         [Zeus lives in a palace on Olympos
               married to Sister Hera
          fucks Semelé
               Cadmos' daughter

                 their child
                   Dionysos
     whom he hides on Crete from Hera's anger]

23.

      where the Kouretes put on their armor
         and danced for him
       [as they did to save his father]

25.

[but Hera found out
     she sent the Titans,   Ge's boys, to kill him]
         they snuck up   amused him with toys
       then   tore him to bits
        ate the result daintily

23.

    these are the toys they used:
    ' pine cone, rhomb, puppets

silver apples from the daughters of Hesperos
who speak with clear voice '
plus a die, sphere, top, mirror,
and fleece

27.

[say this about the Titans]

the Purification from frankincense

Titans

shining children
of Skyheaven & Earth
fathers before
of our fathers

Titans

beneath Earth
in the wombs of Tartaros

tending the wells
that feed dying men
whom pain never frees

Titans

of saltsea
of wingbirdair
of earthhome

please
keep your anger away
if one of you comes to my house

25.

          Zeus found out what they did
              he smashed them with a thunderbolt

        from the soot of the smoke of their bombing
           he made the stuff we're remade of:

28.

                 the Titanic Race: us
               part cannibal
               part light

     whom Zeus taught
      worse things than Phanes and Kronos
        taught their folk :

                    ' plan ahead
                         get it right '
Golden Silver Titanic: these are all the kinds there are

25.

             part Titan
              part Dionysos
                  so   don't kill yourself
             —you can't anyway—
             the body is not a prison
               despite what they say:
                   soma/sema

29.

     [life and death: no difference
       you can always make a comeback
         remember:]

      ' birds & beasts &
             the guilt-ridden tribes of men '
hermeneutic: beasts and birds/ the consumed nations of man

     ' the burdens of earth
                hammered out bodies
                         nothing through nothing '
   hermeneutic: the onus of earth/ made-up bodies
                nothing is born   nothing dies

26.

Zeus couldn't get over his boy's death
                made a plaster statue of him in Crete
  put in it the heart Sister Athené had saved from the Titans
     right where   he'd framed the lineaments of the chest

          for tomb built him a temple
                his pedagogue Silenus the priest

  Cretans
        to soften his pain and theirs
              keep his deathday holy
          every third year   sacred
    doing again in order everything Dionysos did
               and suffered when he died
      they chew up a living bull
    they race through the woods
         crying out his name
           real
        there is no pretense
     endless chanting dancing ecstasy
  flutes scream
         cymbals smash
 a top whirling on a string
        recalls the bull's hoarse bellow

     bacchants carry the box Athené put his heart in
      and the toys that beguiled him

this is how a god who couldn't be buried was made

30.

[sing this song for] Zeus

	:	first
	:	last
	:	lashing lightning thunder thunder flash
Zeus	:	head
	:	body of
everything that is	:	
	:	cock
	:	cunt
	:	stand of the bowl of earth of sky of stars
	:	King
Zeus	:	who does it all
one	:	dyne
	:	demon
	:	kingbody of everything wheeling into one
	:	night day
Zeus	:	Metis first and subtlest (mist of) air
Zeus	:	Eros who is every delight don't fight his powerflesh
face	:	lightpricked sky

beard	:	gold glare stars hung in air
		          two gold bull's horns
		                flashing right and left

	:	sunrise & set
	:	walkway of the gods of sky
eyes	:	sun and measuring/answering moon
mind	:	that does not deceive royal FireAir that does not wear out

everything : listens
           : bows to him

he : notes   purposes   points

ear : that hears
      your voice cry shout doomscream

Zeus : deathless head
       : untiring thought

body : muscles of light no end
      at peace dauntless strong boned

shoulders   chest   back : air hissing everywhere
         his wings span out
      so that he is absent nowhere

stomach : earthmotherall   mountain crests
       puckered ocean sea ruffling
waist and belt :

feet : fixed deep in roots
      in moldy pit
      Earth's buried anchor

Zeus : who swallows all
     : to once anew bring out in cheerful
dayfather[mother] :

     : planting again enroots his godbody

An alternate conclusion for *Sacred Stories* taken from the *Clementine Homilies*. This follows the withdrawal of Phanes into Night's cave.

Lady Hyle
 now a hollow nook
  lay down under Chronos/'Olam
   submitting to time
 he filled her up again

she "turned" curdled
  boiling with children

1. Pluto king of the dead
   who is heavy sank down beneath Earth
   whom Chronos/'Olam swallowed
    all of him
     rough and dirty
  for that is his return his recession

2. Poseidon who is water
   whatever floats to the surface of Lady Hyle

3. Zeus clear fire
   whom Chronos/'Olam could not swallow
    for he climbed into Skyheaven
     rolling up like a ball doing somersaults
  burning off the wet
    drinking it and breathing out
    made Metis subtlest [mist of] wind
from/on a crest of FireAir which he bit off and swallowed
    he shaped Pallas
     the Ball Player
      Balloter
      Palper
  whose mindedness he needed to make the world

from jabbing Zeus from burning Fire
  Air reached the place they call Hera

Sister because Air is so clear
Wife because as in woman Fire can only come in Air

BIBLIOGRAPHY FOR *SACRED STORIES*

Numbers on left-hand side of text correspond to those assigned the fragments below. All fragments found in: Kern, *Orphicorum Fragmenta* (*OF*).

1. Malalas, *Chronography, OF* #62
2. Ibid., *OF* #65
3. 'Apion' as quoted in the *Clementine Homilies, OF* #56
4. Lactantius, *Divine Institutes, OF* #89
5. Quoted in Proclos, *On Plato's Timaios, OF* #85
6. Hermias, *On Plato's Phaedrus, OF* #76
7. Ibid., *OF* #105
8. Summarized from *OF* #98
9. Proclos, *On Plato's Timaios, OF* #104
10. Condensed from *OF* #109
11. *Orphic Hymn VII, OF* #100
12. Quoted in Proclos, *On Plato's Timaios, OF* #114
13. Proclos, *On Hesiod's Works and Days, OF* #130
14. Eustathius, *Guide to Dionysos, OF* #115
15. Summarized from Hesiod's *Theogony*
16. Porphyry, *The Cave of the Nymphs, OF* #154. Also see Proclos, *On Plato's Cratylos, OF* #137
17. Quoted in Proclos, *On Plato's Cratylos, OF* #127
18. Proclos, *On Plato's Timaios, OF* #164
19. Ibid., *OF* #165
20. Ibid., *OF* #166
21. Ibid., *OF* #167
22. Ibid., *OF* #167
23. Clement of Alexandria, *Protreptica* (*Exhortations*), *OF* #34
24. Proclos, *On Plato's Timaios, OF* #85
25. Olympiodoros, *On Plato's Phaedo, OF* #220
26. Firmicus Maternus, *The Errors of Profane Religion, OF* #214
27. *Orphic Hymn 38, OF* #220
28. Proclos, *On Plato's Republic, OF* #140
29. Malalas, *Chronography, OF* #76
30. Quoted by Porphyry in Eusebius, *Preparation for the Gospel, OF* #168
31. Proclos, *On Plato's Timaios, OF* #107

FROM APOLLONIUS OF RHODES,

THE ARGONAUTICA

A Greek text of the third century B.C. from the *Argonautica* of Apollonius of Rhodes. Text: Diels-Kranz, *Die Fragmente der Vorsokratiker,* Vol. 1.

Orpheus picked up his lyre

    " Earth & Sea & Sky

           who once were One

      Hate split up

these are the eternal reminders

                stars
                moon
                sun paths

      then the mountains rose

          the rivers sang
             to the nymphs in their streams
               who answered their song

      was born the creeping the crawling
             whoever goes on all fours

Ophion Snake &
        Eurynomé wide ruler
           on snow topped Olympos

        he like Kronos in his hand's force
             she like Rhea

           but they fell into Ocean's waves

then Kronos and Rhea
           were lords of the Titans

   Zeus still young

      still child thinking in Dicté's cave

not yet made strong by thunder lightning
              and lightning flash

       which the Cyclops gave him
         to give him glory "

FROM THE *ORPHIC ARGONAUTICA*

A Greek text, c. second century A.D. Text: *Orphic Argonautica*
11.419–32, in Kern, *Orphicorum Fragmenta #29.*

I picked up my lyre
song came
flooding my mouth
        first the black song of old Chaos
                who barters birth
           then Sky coming to limit
           Earth with her wide teats
                sea sounding the deeps
        oldest self-beginning ending wily Love

                everything was born
                    everything pulled apart
              from one another

       Kronos the Destroyer

                    Zeus who loves thunder

       kings of the gods who never do without

I sang of the birth of the younger armed gods

     who argued (with the Titans)

          the Titans who rent Brimos Bacchos:

          the populous birth of feeble men

throughout the narrow cave
the song of my lyre
coursing through the honeyed voice

Elemental Creation

II.   FALLING

FROM ARISTOPHANES, *THE BIRDS*

A Greek text by Aristophanes, c. fifth century B.C.; the cosmogony here dates back to c. 1000 B.C. Text: Aristophanes, *The Birds,* in Kern, *Orphicorum Fragmenta* #1.

first   Gap   Night   deep Dark   abyss Tartaros

               no air earth or sky

then in deep Dark's bottomless wombs
Night on black wings laid the wind egg

as the seasons went round
        there hatched Love the Desired
    who shoots light forth
     from the gold wings on his back
     who has the body of wind turned on tornado spins

at night he blended in Gap down below in abyss Tartaros
       laying/hatching the eggs of our race
           he first led us to light

before Love mixed in
       there were no deathless gods
once he had let everything go
       into everything else
   sea sky air
      as well as the gods' imperishable race
           were born

A Latin text by Hyginus, c. first century B.C./A.D., taken from traditional Near Eastern sources dating back to c. 1400 B.C. Text: Hyginus, *Fabulae* (Rose, ed.).

a giant egg fell into the Euphrates

fish pushed it to shore

where doves sat down and warmed it

it hatched

out came Venus

later called the Syrian Goddess

(Ashtaroth)

THREE MIDRASHIM

FROM THE *PIRKE DE RABBI ELIEZER*

From the Hebrew text *Pirke de Rabbi Eliezer,* c. A.D. 150.
Text: *Pirke de Rabbi Eliezer,* ed. Zisberg and Halter.

.   .   .   .   .   .

created 8 things the first day

sky	light	tohu	wind
earth	dark	bohu	water

"& the *wind* of Elohim moved on the *water*"

(1)

THE ORIGIN OF SKY

was from light of his own robe
he took & stretched it
like a robe the skies
were rolling out from
he figured that should do it
in Shadai's words   "shall do"
—became his name then—
then firmed it up (they say)
"thy covering of thyself
"with light
"is like a robe
"the way thou stretchest the sky out
" 's like a curtain"

(2)

THE ORIGIN OF EARTH

took snow or ice
—'twas underneath his throne—
& dropped it on
the waters
then they became congealed
earth's crust was formed from it
(they say)
"he tells the snow
"be earth"

(3)

COSMOLOGIES

sky's curtain hooks 're set in
ocean's water
's set between the ends of
sky & earth
the ends of sky 're spread across
his ocean's waters
"are his house posts set into
"his waters"

. . . .

that we should see the sky from inside
—& call it dome—
was like a basket
maybe like a tent
stretched out & with the tent flaps
downward
the dome stretched high & far
the people crowd in
feet set on the earth
& everyone inside the tent
the way the sky's ends

touch the earth
dome stretches upward
& all life's lived
inside it
like a tent (they say)
"he spreads them like a tent
"to dwell in"

. . . .

4 winds or quarters
made for earth
1 east
1 south
1 west
1 north
from the quarter facing east
light seeks the world
from the quarter facing south
sweet dew   sweet rain
from the quarter facing west
the treasuries of snow & hail
bring cold & heat into the world
& hard rain
from the quarter facing north
darkness moves out
"fourth quarter's incomplete (he says)
"made but unfinished
"anyone who says he's god
"can come & work on it
"complete it
"then everyone will say
"this one's a god"

FROM THE FIFTH ELEGY OF MAXIMIAN

From the Fifth Elegy of Maximian of Etruria who lived c.
A.D. 600 and holds the distinction of being the last pagan Latin
poet. Text: in Bährens, ed., *Poetae Latini Minores,* Vol. 5.

cock holidays busy plowing
cock   wealth   joy   giver
I weep for you
          lost in a whirl of tears
although no song I have
is worth you

when I burned
tidal fire bursting my soul
you soothed
giving me a game to play

guard who never slept
but made do with me
          whether I laughed or cried

with my secrets
and their secret resting place
I trusted you
standing straight and true
in internal service
all night long

who did it?
made you lose the feeling power?
when will you lift your coxcomb
to stab me again?

now soft and bloodless
you bow to death

I am helpless to touch you into life
sing you into me

you look ready for the grave

rightly said :
"what no longer does dies"
. . .

his failing
not my loss
but everyone's
chaos come back again

cock made people cattle bird and beast
on this globe whatever breathes

take him away
male and female die
man's mind not join woman's
in union that makes their bodies one

take him away
lovely woman loses her price
the men go for nothing

there's no sun-bit gold
                    in a crystalled gem

dead cock cheats
like a farm sown with salt
working towards death

but cock live
then we trust ourselves
we keep our secrets safe and holy

come cock
joy today
a future tomorrow

the universe is yours
the Kings above   below
chose to give you their rods
surrendering to joy
they do not lie
                    groveling at your feet

. . .

ever since the gods
drove the giants from the sky
cock you throw the triple-sheeted lightning bolt
                              for angered Zeus

teaching the tigress love
and the lion kindness

even Wisdom, this world's Queen
gives you her hand
obeying your commands

equally strong and patient
you amaze
those you've beaten
you love yet
you enjoy losing
lying down in defeat
once more to rise loving
again to lose to win

Elemental Creation

III. DIVIDING

Autonomic and Aliyan Texts

A. Autonomic Texts

DAMASCIUS,

THE EGYPTIAN COSMOLOGY

The Egyptian Cosmology according to Damascius; a Greek text, c. A.D. 500, from an Egyptian source, c. 500 B.C. Text: Damascius, *De Principiis* (Ruelle, ed.).

one

one who is called by the name of unknown shadows

(say three times)

two

Water and Sand

or Sand and Water

their child

KA-ME[M?]PHIS I
[Ptah?]

father of

KA-ME[M?]PHIS II
[Isis?]

father of

KA-ME[M?]PHIS III
[Horus?]

they are the world   the diacosm

AN INCANTATION AGAINST TOOTHACHE

An Akkadian cosmogony attached to an incantation in order to assure control, c. 800 B.C. Text: *Cuneiform Texts from Babylonian Tablets, etc., in the British Museum.*

Start:

Sky made sky
sky made dirt
dirt made flow-ers
flow-ers made canals
canals made swamp

swamp made worm

From *De Principiis* by Damascius, a Greek text, c. A.D. 500, from a Babylonian source, c. 1000 B.C. Text: *De Principiis* (Ruelle, ed.).

there are two
{ TAUTHÉ   { APASON
{ (Tiamat)   and { (Apsu)

{ TAUTHÉ
{ (Tiamat)   mother of the gods
{ APASON
{ (Apsu)   her lover

their child { MOYMIS—who is everything we see
{ (Mummu)

and then they had
{ DACHÉ   and { DACHOS
{ (Laḫmu)   and { (Laḫamu)

and then
{ KISSARÉ   and { ASSOROS
{ (Kišar)   { (Anšar)
and they had three children
{ ANOS
{ (Anu)

{ ILLINOS
{ (Enlil)

{ AOS
{ (Ea)

{ AOS' and { DAUKÉ'S   son: { BELOS   the Maker
{ (Ea)   { (Damkinna)   { (BEL)
                             { (Marduk)

SANCHUNIATHON,

THE *PHOENICIAN HISTORY*

A Greek translation, c. second century A.D., translated into Greek by Philo of Byblos from the works of the Phoenician poet, Sanchuniathon, who lived, possibly in Byblos as well, c. 1300–900 B.C. The present fragmentary text is found in: Eusebius, *Praeparatio Evangelica*, in *Patrologia Graeca*, Migne (ed.).

Prefaces by various hands

Eusebius, *Preparation for the Gospel* (Fourth century A.D.)

The gods, according to the ancients, are representations of our moral nature and, in the words of the oracle, the invention of images for them marked the beginning of their disappearance. But this is not true: in point of fact the gods, having sprung or rather initiating from the Phoenicians and the Egyptians, passed from them to other nations —in particular to the Greeks. That this is true is confirmed by the history it is now time for us to review: the Phoenician "testament."

Porphyry, *Against the Christians* (Third century A.D.)

The truest history of the Semitic peoples is contained in that Sanchuniathon of Beirut because his most closely agrees with the topology and onomastics of the region. Furthermore he used as raw material the records of Hierobalus, the priest of Ieuo [pronounced "Yeh-woh"], and dedicated his book to Adibalos, the king of Beirut, since it had been approved by the king and his scholars. These men lived before the Trojan War, almost about the time Moses did, as the Phoenician king-lists show. Sanchuniathon, who fell in love with his subject, collected and wrote his work from the records of the local cities in Phoenicia and from the priestly registers. It is further said he lived during the reign of Semiramis, the Assyrian queen whom the chroniclers tell us flourished either before the time of the Trojan War or else was its contemporary. And this is the History that Philo of Byblos translated into Greek.

Philo of Byblos: *Translator's Preface* (Second century A.D.)

Sanchuniathon, a man of great learning and desirous of still more knowledge, interested himself in the early history of all peoples, beginning from the creation of the world. Painstakingly he researched the history of Taautos since he knew full well that of all men born under the sun Taautos was the only inventor of letters and record keeping. With him, as most appropriate, he began his *History:* with him whom the Egyptians call Thoyth, the Alexandrians Thoth, and the Greeks Hermes.

But the most recent of hierologues who reject the real even before they begin to write, treating of one thing in the guise of another, have striven to invent a fabulous mythology. They do not stop at this, but even shape imaginary analogues between this world and the conditions of the cosmos, establishing mysteries and wrapping everything in a cloud of darkness and ignorance so that one cannot easily find out the truth of what in fact did take place. But Sanchuniathon, who happened upon the writings of the Ammoneans, composed secretly in their temples (and naturally not known to all men), set to work to master them. Having done that, he was able to write and, most importantly, to put away the received myths and their attendant allegories. However, the priests who came later, wishing to restore the mythic character, swathed his *History* in silence and obscurity, whereupon the mystic sense arose, even among the Greeks, it not having touched them previously.

For the sake of explaining the *History* itself and its contents, it is necessary to make clear right from the start that the ancient barbarians, principally the Phoenicians and the Egyptians (from whom the rest of the world received their traditions), worshipped as gods whatever contributed to the health and well-being of communal life. In particular it was the Phoenicians' habit to affix their kings and whoever among them divinely conspicuous to the elements of the cosmos, but they knew no other gods than those of the natural world, sun, moon, and the other wandering stars (all that has grown out of connection with them), so that some of their gods are mortal and others are not.

I. *Creation*

All father Ruaḥ Air, dark blowing clouding
a wind a cloud : and Gap Koḥot'erev chaos black as Erebos
swirling in gloom throughout that first long age,
boundless endless

Ruaḥ falls in love with his parts
sprays himself with come
Hipeḥ, Desire
beginning things
though Ruaḥ did not know it yet,
the child of himself : Mot
whom some call mud
and others mold, from her
zera' the spores of creation the genetices of the world,
then there were others :
the ḥayot not possessed of sense,
from them the Tzofe-šemin who were,
and Mot the Egg burst into light
and the sun and the moon and the stars and the big ones

w h e n s h e h a d b u r s t i n t o l i g h t

      ' s splendor

her strong

        heat

struck

      land

        and

          sea

           ,

               clouded

      blew

rained

      they stood apart

      each moved from their place

      from the blow of her heat

      and flew up back into Ruaḥ

    meeting rubbing

              crushing together

                    thunder lightning flash

    at that noise

    the Tzofe-šemin awake

and were frightened

and began to move out on the land and sea male and female

II. *The Nomoi*

from the Wind that blows from the Gulf
from Qol-pias and Baau his wife
the first diers
Hava and Adam Qadmun
Aion and Protogonos
Hava found out
how to eat the fruit of trees

from them
in Phoenicia
their children Qen and Qenat
Birth and Tribe
who in drought
stretch forth their hands
to the sun
master of the sky:
calling him Ba'al-šamin
Day Father

from them N'er, 'Eš, Lahav
Light, Fire, Flame:
from the rubbing of sticks
and teaching the use of it

from them
Nefilim the Titans
and the mountains they name
correspond in size:
Qasiun, Lebanun, Hermun, Tabor

from them
Šame-merom/Hypsuranios and 'Esav/Beš
named for their mothers:
as women then
fucked without shame
any they met

Šame-merom
lived in Tyre
building huts
of reed and papyrus strands

he quarreled with 'Esav
his brother: who wore
the clothes of the beasts
he caught and skinned

Then it rained in Tyre:
the wind drove the trees
against each other
and made them burn
and so the place
was stripped of wood

Though 'Esav
catching a tree
lopped the branches off
and paddled out to sea:
the first

And dedicating two pillars
to Wind and Fire:
poured the blood of the beasts
he caught over them

from their children:
Šet and Sidon
man of the wilds
man of the seas:
the hunting and fishing clans

from them
the Iron Worker
Kothar:
singer enchanter speaker diviner
Hephaistos:
fashioner of the hook, bait, line, and raft
who were worshipped
once they died:

god of the trades and clans/ Malak the Worker
and his brother
built walls of brick

from Worker's people
Qen the Technites
and Autochthon
Adam Landsman

they chopped straw
mixed clay
cut it into bricks
dried in the sun
result: roofs

from them Šet and Sadé
Tiller and Stalker:
Stalker is
the great god of Byblos:
in Phoenicia they still carry
his statue
on an oxcart:
they built houses
with basements and courtyards
and rooms

from them 'Ilim and Nefilim
Farmers and Hunters
called Settlers and Nomads

their children
Amynos and Magos
Upright and Wise
built villages
and herded sheep

their children
Mish'or the Busy and Tzadoq the Just
discovered salt

from Mishor
Taaut
inventor of the alphabet:
whom the Egyptians call Thoyth
the Alexandrians Thoth
and the Greeks Hermes
three times master

from Tzadoq
the Dioskouroi or Cabeiroi or Corybantes or Samothraces:
the Kabirim who built the first ship
whose children
the first to pick herbs
cured snake bite
weaving charms from them

And in that time
lived 'Elion the "most high"
and his lady, Berut/Ba'alat
their home was Byblos

III. *The 3 Generations*

Adam Landsman
they called Uranos Shama
from the excellence
of his beauty
he names the upper world

Adamat Ge
his sister
naming the lower
the Earth

'Elion died
meeting beasts
and became a god:
his children poured out
and fed him
according to the rites

144   ORIGINS

Adam
king in his place
married Adamat
and had by her:
'El
who is Kronos: and
Bet-'el: and
Dagon
who is Wheat Food God: and
Atlas Anatal(?)

Adam married
many times and had
many children by the concubines of heaven:

Adamat took that bitterly
and struck back with hard words
so they parted

Adam
came back
and filled her with children
by force and went away
whenever it was his mood
destroying them
when he could

many times
Adamat drove him back
gathering friends
about her
'El and Taaut
his secretary
protected her
and saved her honor

the children of 'El:
Persephoné 'Elat
that died virgin:
Athené 'Anat
who with Taaut

told him to forge
the iron sickle
and the iron spear

Taaut spoke
magic to the 'Elohim
the cronies of 'El:
wrought desire in them
to fight against Adam

and:
overthrew his father
seizing the kingship

they took
the lovely concubine
of Adam in that battle:
she carried his son
in her belly, but 'El
gave her in marriage
to Dagon, and in his house
she bore him Demarous
who is Ba'al Tamar

'El built a wall
around his house:
Byblos in Phoenicia,
the first city

He grew suspicious
of his brother Atlas
and threw him in a pit:
he listened to Taaut
and buried him

Then the children
of the Kabirim
ran their ships aground
at the foot of Mt. Qasiun
and built a temple there

'El killed his son Šadid
and cut off the head
of one of his daughters
with the iron sword:
he had no trust in them
he surprised all the gods
by his mindedness

Adam sent Astarté
and her two sisters
Amma Rhea and Dioné Ba'alt
to kill 'El
by their cunning:
but he fucked them
though his sisters
and married them

when Adam heard
he sent Heimarmené/Giddé
and Hora/No'ema to make war:
but 'El assimilated them
he kept them by his side

Then Adam created Bet'yl
the Baetylia
thinking to put life
into stones

to 'El:
seven daughters by Astarté,
Tanit the Titanides or Artemides:
seven sons by Rhea,
the youngest a god from birth:
and by Dioné girls:
and by Astarté the boys:
Pothos and Eros, Hipeḥ and Dūd

to 'El
by other women
in the Land beyond the River (Euphrates?):
three sons,

'El Again
Zeus/HaBa'al
and Reshef/Apollo

Dagon invented
the plow to furrow
the wheat field:
they called him
" a r o t r i o s "
"the plowman"

Tzadoq married one of the Tanit:
Asclepios/Ešmun
his child

At the same time
Yam and Tzefon
Pontos and Typhoon:
and Nereus/Nahar
HaBa'al's son
Yam's brother

And from Yam
Sidon her voice
so lovely in song
there came music forth

And from Yam
Tan/Poseidon
lord of the sea

Ba'al Tamar's son:
Mel-kart who is the (Tyrian) Herakles

then afterward:
Adam fought with Yam
Ba'al Tamar helped

Ba'al Tamar jumped into Yam
but Yam ran away

Ba'al Tamar said
"if I get away
I'll give you something to eat"

And in the 32nd year
of his kingship
inland
beside springs and brooks
'El caught his father
and tore out his balls
with his own hands:
Adam became god there
as breath left him
blood trickling down
drop by drop from the wound
into those springs and brooks,
today I could show you the spot

This is the story of Adam and all his people

The first and golden age of men: *meropes*

"who speak with clear articulate voice"

---

as the poets write

---

that blessed happiness of an ancient time

Astarté, the greatest
of goddesses, and Ba'al Tamar/Adonis
and Hadad
king of the gods
became lords of Phoenicia
'El approved

Astarté set a bull's head upon her own
as the sign of her power
circling the earth
she found a star fallen to earth
which she gave to Tyre
and consecrated on that holy isle

her name
the Phoenicians say
is also Aphrodite

'El in his journeyings
gave the queenship
of Attica to Anat

when the plague came
and death:
'El offered Adam
his only son burnt whole
he cut off the tip of his penis
forcing the 'Elohim
to do the same

when his son by Rhea
Mot died
he made him god:
to signify death to the Phoenicians
the Greeks call him
T h a n a t o s P l u t o

'El gave his city Byblos
to the goddess Baaltis
whom the Greeks call Dioné
and Berytos to Tan
and the Kabirim: to both
the Farmers and the Sailors

of Yam
what they found:
they made god
in Berytos

Taaut before this
imitated the shapes
of Adam and the other gods:
of 'El and Dagon:
of all those who were with Adam
he struck the sacred stamp:
he gave to letters
their character

for 'El
he made the Seal of Kingship
four eyes that look
to the front and four behind
two of them closed in sleep
and two open on each side:
upon his shoulders
he set four wings
two spread in flight
two folded in rest
and the Seal reads,
'El sees and sleeps
sleeps and sees
flies at rest
rests in flight:
to each
of the other gods
he gave two wings
since they fly with 'El

to 'El
he gave two more wings
and put them on his head
one for the quality
of his mindedness
the other
for swiftness
of his thought

when 'El
came to the land
of the South Wind
he gave Taaut
for palace
the whole of Egypt

. . .

All this
the seven sons of Tzadoq
the Kabirim preserved

and their eighth brother
Ešmun as the god
Taaut told them to

IV. ['Olam] the Dragon Snake

Taaut made the dragon snake god
                        breath spirit and fire
                body so quick
                        you cannot see it
                though he has no hands or feet

spirals
        where he's going
                taking   leaving shape

                                never dies
                        sheds his skin
                        becoming young
                                renews his age

                                ready to die
                        he swallows himself

                        you want to kill him?
                cut him first into pieces
                        otherwise you never will

        they call him ⎰AGATHODAIMON the ⎰MALAKH   Ba'al
                       ⎱PrettyDemon   ⎱angel of

ALCMAN 5 FRAGMENT 2 ii, COLUMN ii

This text was originally discovered on a papyrus scrap in Egypt in 1957. It contains a commentary (in fragmentary form) by an unknown scholar c. third century B.C. on a now-lost cosmological poem by Alcman, a poet active in the eighth–seventh centuries B.C., who was born in Lydia in Asia Minor and worked mainly in Sparta. Text: in *Poetae Melici Graeci*, (Page, ed.). "[. . .]" denotes lost words supplied by papyrologists; ". . ." denotes lost letters; "x" denotes letter x has been restored; "x-y" denotes two possible readings, x or y; "/" denotes a full stop; "(. . .)" denotes translator's additions or explanatory words; "?" denotes a supposition; word or words in *italics* means it is being quoted by the ancient commentator from Alcman's lost original.

. . .

. n . [
of all . . . [
someone-a *out of the p*[si
gn was born t[
mo[.] and then-from (sign?) ei . [(was born?)
way (a word which is derived) from way- . [. .] . [(making?)
for when unwrought timber stuff began to be shape[d
(by the skills of Thetis??)
a way as if (for) a start was born / indeed Alcman s[ays

the unwrought timberstuff of every[thing-one was in dis
array and lacked finished form / next someone [was bo
rn, he says, who bu[ilt and furnished
everything-one / next (he says) [w]ay was born, [and while w
ay was passing by, sign follow[ed] closely in understanding com
pliance / now way really is the beginning as it were, while si
gn (acts as the) end-completion (of extant possibility) /
after (sea mother) Thetis was
born, (way and sign, the) beginning and end-comp[l]etio[n thes]e
(two) of everything-one, w
ere bo[r]n / and indeed the everything-one has a nature-(from)-birth

(which is) [the sa]me as
the unwrought timberstuff of copper
(or: of all metals before iron: bronze, brass, etc.), while
Thetis (was) i[ts] artificer-shaper, and way and si
gn (worked as) beginning and end-completion /
(in this poem Alcman uses the form) *oll[d maan]*

---

instead of the (usual word for) old man /
(he says) *and third shadowdarkness*

---

because neither sun nor m
o]on had yet been born since (at that time)
t]he unwrought timberstuff (of everything-one)
was still unpart[e]d-unmingl[e]d / indeed
              under-by-from . [.] . . w
ay and sign and shadowdark[ness] were born . / [*day*

---

and moon and third shadowdarkness / the
flashings-sparklings-glancing glitterdartings (of stars?) /
day (was) not (born) all by herself but
(at the same time-by the same act) as (the) sun /
for previously shadowdarkness lived (all) alo
ne, but afterwards when he'd been part[e]d-mixedandmingl[e]d

FROM THE *HOMERIC ALLEGORIES*
OF HERACLITOS THE GRAMMARIAN

A Greek text by Heraclitos the Grammarian, c. 30 B.C.–
c. A.D. 14. Provenance unknown. Text: *Héraclite: Allégories
d'Homère* (Buffière, ed.), 62.

sometime long ago before the ForeMother set out the Wholes
                    and gave them roots

when what was not had not yet had its character struck
or else lay blanketed under mere-slime
since she had not picked out Types
to imprint her young impressionables
or driven a center spike deep into Earth her Wholes' vestal heart
spinning Sky on it to secure his swift changeless fruitful rush

when everything was   sunless desert   downcast soundless night
things-not-things   unfilled
by the still empty MotherTimberStuff
for this was a slack time her lovely bodyforms had yet to employ

then WorldMother Start worked everything into her fashion
drawing them for safety and health into her body
to give them birth
she bore the universe her beauty's/*cosmos* which is also order
unhooked earth from sky unfurled endless land and sea
untangling them from each other
for her self's adorning arranged 4 Rows
the 4 Roots that bear the Wholes
in fore-thought/clusters that re-produce
the well-turned features of her Nature

after she'd considered everything
before shuffling each into place
the god . . . since she had no clear choice
separated into shape her once aimless body . . .

DAMASCIUS, THE IRANIAN COSMOGONY

A Greek text by Damascius, c. A.D. 500, from an Iranian source, c. third century A.D. Text: Damascius, *De Principiis* (Ruelle, ed.).

everything you see   PLACE   or

TIME

which separate in Two

making a double pair

OROMESDES   who is   Light
Ahura-Mazda

AREIMANIOS   who is   Dark
Ariman

PLACE
Topos

————Zerauné akerené

TIME
Chronos

FROM THE 36TH *DISCOURSE*
OF DIO CHRYSOSTOM

A Greek text, c. first century A.D., taken from a Persian source
after the fifth century B.C. Text: Dio Chrysostom, *Discourses*
(H. Crosby, ed.), Vol. V.

Everybody knows the Sun has a chariot
                            but what about Zeus's?
                                  his is much older
                        yet not a word about it in Homer or Hesiod

        Zoroaster knew
                    he had a song which he taught the Magi

                            alone on a mountain
                        he lived in his love of wisdom

        then the mountain burned
                        fire falling from the sky
                                never stopping
                the shah and his court came to witness

the prophet stepped out of the sheath of flame unhurt
                        "I'm all right
                            you should be too
                    burn food for the god who's come here"

        Zoroaster went into the world
                    and lived with the Wise: the Magi
                    whom he showed the demonic

        they are not magicians as the Greeks say

                    for Zeus they keep a team of Nisaean horses
                        the best and biggest in Asia
                        but for the Sun—just one horse

The Story of the Horses and the World

think the diacosm a 4 horse chariot drawn along a single road
by the highest driver who does   and   knows
no stopping no ending his driving
an eternal turning in time
Sun and Moon only partial to the whole
so people see them
but they're partials too
the diacosm's moving and circling
most never notice
because the struggle's so great

the four Horses

first: Aither
on the outside runs the longest track
big beautiful fast
Zeus's favorite
wings color of fire of spotless light
Sun Moon other stars piebalds on his hide
sparks in clusters flying rippling
in close night

some in formation
others off by themselves
dancing slapping against each other

loners: the planets
the troupes: constellations
figures schematic form patterns

second: Hera/Air
who obeys is gentle weak and slow
black
but bright where Sun strikes
otherwise in shadow
turns to find color

third: Poseidon/Water
                         slower than Hera

          once he came down   the poets say
                                  his image Pegasos
                         hoof pawed earth a fountain leapt up
                         Spring Peirené at Corinth
                                        still there
                                        you can see it

fourth: Hestia/Earth
                              who does not move has no wings
               (don't ask me to explain
                              certain things just can't be
               besides this is a story)

                         hitched to the chariot
                              he stands still
                    chewing the iron bit
          Hera and Poseidon bend toward him pushing and crowding
               but Aither farthest away
                              always rounds him first
                    while he holds steady as a turning post
                              in the hippodrome

YAHVIST GENESIS

The Hebrew cosmogony of the J-E tradition, c. 2000–700 B.C.
Text: Kittel, *Biblia Hebraica,* Gen. 2.4b–.23.

When Yahweh of the gods was making earth and skies

> not even a wild bush existed on earth
> not even a wild grass had come up

> since Yahweh of the gods hadn't made rain on earth
> since no Landman was to work the earth

> water'd just gush from the earth
> and water 'cross the whole land

Yahweh of the gods shaped landman from lumps of land, and blew the soft-blowing wind of life into his nostrils. So then landman was breathing life. Then Yahweh of the gods planted a garden on a pleasant plain in the east, and put the landman he'd shaped there. Then Yahweh of the gods raised every tree worth looking at and worth eating from, and in the middle of the garden is the tree of immortality and the tree of knowing-what's-good-and-bad. A river comes up in the plain to water the garden, then splits into four branches: one of them is the Hopper, winding through all of the Havila country, where the gold is—good gold at that—and bdellium and lapis lazuli; the second river's name is Gusher—that's the one that winds all through the Kassite country; the name of the third river is Tigris, which runs east of Ashur; and the fourth is the Euphrates.

Anyway, Yahweh of the gods took landman and put him in the garden on the pleasant plain to work it and watch it. Then Yahweh of the gods commanded the landman: "You can eat from any of the trees of the garden except the tree of knowing-what's-good-and-bad. If you eat from that one, you're doomed from then on."

So then Yahweh of the gods said to himself, "It's not good landman being alone. I'll make him the right helper."

So
from the land
Yahweh of the gods shaped
all the wild animals
all the birds of the skies

Then he brought them to the landman to see what he'd call them.
Whatever the landman called them is their name.

So
the landman gave names
to every bird of the skies
to every wild life

But he didn't find a fit helper for the landman. So Yahweh of
the   gods put the landman into a deep sleep. When he was asleep, he
took one of his ribs then closed the flesh back up. Then Yahweh of the
gods built the rib he'd taken from the landman into a woman, and
brought her to the landman, who sang:

"That's the one
a bone from my bones
a flesh from my flesh

This one will be called woman
'Cause she's taken from a   man."

That's why a man'll leave his father and mother: to hang around
his woman, because they're one flesh.

THE PHOENICIAN COSMOGONY
ACCORDING TO MOCHOS

The Phoenician cosmogony according to Mochos, a Greek text, c. A.D. 500; taken from a Phoenician source, c. ninth–eighth century B.C. (after Sanchuniathon). Text: Damascius, *De Principiis* (Ruelle, ed.).

he-Fire   she-Air

their son ⌠'OLAM
        ⌡Chronos

who makes love to himself

his son ⌠CHUSOROS the Egg-Opener
     ⌡[Phanes?]

next Egg

below them the Winds in degree

Wind: Ruaḥ

Winds: ⌠LIPS and ⌠NOTOS
      ⌡Libyan   ⌡["fatherless"?]

Egg is ⌠SKY
      ⌡Uranos

for when Egg hatched

the half shells became   sky and earth

THEOGONY FROM SIDON

From the Phoenician city of Sidon, a Greek text, c. A.D. 500, taken from a Greek source, Eudemos (fourth century B.C.) reporting a Phoenician source from the eighth–seventh century B.C. Text: Damascius, *De Principiis* (Ruelle, ed.). ". . ." denotes words omitted.

{ CHRONOS
{ 'Olam

then { POTHOS   and   { OMICLÉ
     { Desire   { Darkness

from these two

the first Two:

                       he-Fire
                       she-Breath

. . .

from the first Two mixing and mingling: { OTÜS
                                            { Egg

Fragment 57 from *Hypsipylé,* a lost play by Euripides, contains one of the oldest of the Orphic cosmogonies, c. 1000 B.C.
Text: Kern, *Orphicorum Fragmenta* #2. "[. . .]" denotes
words supplied.

. . . [Night]

you who rule the gods

[mother of] ⎰ LOVE the unseen demanding ⎰ LIGHT
         ⎱ Eros   ⎱ [Phanes?]

child you bore first to fireair . . .

THE COSMIC OUTLINE OF ACUSILAUS

This cosmological summary, c. A.D. 500, was abstracted from the works of the Greek poet Acusilaus, c. seventh–sixth century B.C. Text: Damascius, *De Principiis* (Ruelle, ed.).

first
Gap the unknown
then

Erebos   Night
he   she
bounded   boundless

their
children:
Aither
Eros
Metis

their
children's
children:
the other gods

FRAGMENTS FROM EPIMENIDES,

THE *BIRTH OF THE GODS* OR *ORACLES*

This Greek text by Epimenides dates from the sixth century
B.C. It contains an Orphic cosmology which goes back probably to at least the seventh or eighth century B.C. Text: in Diels-
Kranz, *Die Fragmente der Vorsokratiker,* Vol. 1. "———"
divides the fragments. "(. . .)" denotes a possibly spurious
fragment.

Moon of lovely hair my mother
                in my house sharing the smoke

        I shuddered and shook the lion
        I met in Nemea and choked
                for Hera

———

first FireAir and Night
             then Pit

          three from two
        mixing and mingling

———

               two from three
              mixing and mingling
                     { TITANS
                     { tighteners
       stretching from top to bottom
                beginning to end

      coming together
              egg
        one
      everyone

———

   I have no stories about what will be
  only what was and then I speak in "if's"

——

there is no navel set in the middle of earth and sea
         anchoring the cord
     or "if" so
    the gods see it
      we don't

——

  (⎰DIO'S ⎰KOUROI were man and woman
   ⎱Zeus' ⎱lads

        he timemaker one

        she earth   two

      from one and two every number

        lives and breathes)

EURIPIDES,

FRAGMENT 6 OF THE *MELANIPPÉ*

This Greek text from a lost play by Euripides dates from the
late fifth century B.C. Text: Nauck, *Tragicorum Graecorum
Fragmenta.*

this is not my story
but one my mother tells

once Sky and Earth were one
then they split in   two

father and mother of all

brought into light
trees
birds
beasts
fish in the sea
race of living men

JUSTIN, *BARUCH*

This Greek text, c. first century A.D., is probably a condensed translation of Justin's Hebrew or Aramaic original, c. A.D. 40–70. Text: Hippolytus, *Refutatio* (Philosophumenon), ed. Wendland.

> *what eye has not seen*
> > *or ear heard*
> > *what has not yet entered heart*

> > > > now hush
> > > give the gift
> > > > of tongue

Heracles Mel-kart drove Geryon's cattle into Scythia
> > fell asleep in the desert
> woke up   horse gone   cattle too
> > > look   search

found SnakeWoman
> from cunt on up a maiden girl
> > but beware the serpent tail below
> > > "seen my horse?"
> > > > "make me"

does so: throws   3 kids in her bag/behind/cunt centering her
> got his horse and cattle back
> > left

that's the world being laid out
> > 3 beginners

> Yahweh Good Pap Priapos Straight Cock Herding Lady's Thing
> who sees what will be before it is

> Elohim the FatherorMother
> > who can't see this
> > > but invisibly
> > is allowed to father himself everywhere

Eden Israel SnakeWoman
      who knows as little as FatherorMother
            but can she feel!
                   thinking twice
                  two body
          cunt up woman
          cunt down snake

they are the roots the fountains
          without &
          thanks to whom nothing everything the way it is
          and continually being made up and taken away

FatherorMother looked at Eden half woman Israel the rest snake
          "got to have her"

     "Elohim
          I want you too
                  just as much
                         more maybe"

bed

love

fuck

children
          the 12 father's angels

           Michael Amen
           (these things says the Amen,
             the faithful and true witness
            the beginning of the creation of God)
               Baruch Gabriel Esaddaios . . .

     the 12 mother's angels

     Babel Achamoth Naas Baal Belias Satan Sael
     Adonaios Leviathon Pharaoh Carcomenos Lathen

the father's are Elohim's   the mother's Eden Israel's

    all of them in the Paradise
        the Lord God planted
        east of Eden
     turned toward her face
      so she could see it
        and see her angel children

  the trees of the garden these angels
         to say one word for another
           the trees are angels

    tree of life : Baruch
    tree of knowledge of good and bad : ᶜSerpent Naas

Paradise is made of the married joy of Elohim and Eden
where their angels enroot earth's loveliest plots

now earth is Eden Israel but not the snake torso
        from cunt above groin in wife body
        gentle and mild to gaze at
        she made man out of her dirt meat

out of snake springs below cunt she took wild beasts animal creation

men and women chain in flesh the love of FatherorMother and Earth

     "take my windair" she says to Adam
      "my fire" he says   to him

     "I give her airwind
      my picture cuts her size" :
          Eden to Eve

    "give her my fire" said   Elohim

  Adam   signed sealed delivered the covenant still endures
    and Eve:
        "we are one   soul and spirit
       and between you"

JUSTIN, "BARUCH"   171

"multiply and divide
        make up by fucking
                the numbers of the dead
        until they even out the living"

Eden Israel dowered her strength on Elohim
                that's why brides give dowries
        because what Eden did is law

mother's angels 4 groups of 3
        that makes four beginners
                each   called a river of Paradise
                        Phison Gehon Tigris Euphrates
hold hands and run the world in Eden's name
        dancing in a circle
                never in one place too long
                        fixing time to change
                appointed places
                their homes

where Phison is hunger is and pain and woe
        what a cheap squad
                you are, Phison

to each part of the four according to their power and nature
                bad times
                rotten plagues

from their bossing and mixing/mingling
                flood rivers
                currents careers
                        what Eden wants
                no stop for breath just keep it up lady
                        people have to be bad
                                it's her way
                        there's evil in the world

Elohim had fixed up Earth for his "little" garden
                but now time for something else
                "will go up into the sky
                        make sure nothing's left out"

father's angels went along

up   up

"goodbye Eden"
"I am earth I can't leave here"
"right—catch you later"

Elohim at the ceiling of sky saw a light above the light he gave
"open the gates for me to know my lord" for I thought I was"
and the light said
"this is the gate of the Lord which the righteous shall enter"
    the gate opened up
Elohim went in
       his angels did not
to Good Dad Cock
          saw *what eye has not seen or ear heard*
               what has not yet entered heart

Yahweh said
    "sit at my right hand"

Elohim asked
        "Lord let me overturn the world I made
           my fire is chained to men to empty skies"
"no bad now
     you are with me
         you and Eden did the world from married joy
            let her own it as she wants to
                  and no longer—
          you stay with me"

Eden Elohim's desert
        felt love die when he went away
            tears in her eyes
               put mother's angels on her side
dress up time for mother whore nature earth
cheap green leaf Eden sleeve
couched open cunt in the universe
draw Elohim down to her with sloe-eyed winks?
her idea
        hasn't worked yet

Elohim mastered by Papa Cock
                never came back

Eden told Babel Aphrodite
           "make the quimin liars
                   undo their wounds
                       pinch out their husbands' Elohim fire
                           he divorced me
              make his flame in men go dead
                    they not know love
                       death heavy in the heart
                     then feeling ugly
             discover inside the pain he burns me with
             driven from their women by adultery and deceit
             hurt as I was hurt by FatherorMother"
she made Naas strong to blind the Elohim in men
to strike at him through them
          for leaving his qwyf Earth voiding his promise to her

because of this he sent down Baruch
to tend his fire in everyone men and women

Baruch in the midst of the angels of Eden (FAILURE)
                in the midst of paradise park
                   (for the garden is the angels
                        where he stood)
said to Adam
       "eat the fruits of all the trees of paradise
          except the tree Naas who knows right from wrong
        listen to the 11 angels of Eden
            for they feel
        but are innocent of law
            of going against it and breaking it
                but not Naas
                  don't hear him"

      cushioning her slice Naas knew Eve
           gave her lie
         made her fig skirts of shame
    he broke the knotty rose in Adam's anus jerked
          and left his water there

quimin fucking for any reason
men holing men
Naas' work
     if you can get it

Elohim sets out good from bad
         he the single of yes and no
on Cock Dad's right
    shows people the way to him

        but by turning out Eden
          he began evil
            in the fire
              he laid in us

next he sent Baruch to Moses (FAILURE)
      his person when he talked to
            the children of Israel
      to bend them to Yahweh
    Naas swam thru Eden's airwind
         squirmed inside Moses and his chosen
           to sod shut the light of Baruch's words
        so they heard him only

   (airwind is Eden fighting fire Elohim fighting back
   inside
   man or woman   doesn't matter)

Baruch to Prophets (FAILURE)
      to warn Elohim in everyone
        "avoid Eden
          and the lie of the world she gives
       just as FatherorMother did"

Naas enjoyed the Prophets ass backwards
sexed them away from Elohim
supposing Eden's airwind in them
they did not choose
Baruch's words Elohim's laws

sent Heracles Mel-kart (FAILURE)
gentile prophet   hooded cock head
"break the 12 mother's angels
set me free"

the 12 Labors he suffered—Lion Hydra Boar etc.:
goy names borrowed and changed from the energy
of Eden's messengers

looked like he cracked them down   he'd won
then Omphalé robed in her sleek skin body
peeled his cock lace back
soothing him of strength
of Baruch's word
Elohim's issue

what did he get instead?
an envelope of flesh
a narrow slot
run by Eden the power below
Heracles Mel-kart your words did not come true
your deeds still need doing

Baruch to Nazareth (AN OUTCOME?)
when Herod was king
to Jesus son of Joseph and Mary
12 years old
tending sheep

told him the story of the world which is just the story
                    of Eden and Elohim
            marrying and divorcing

and about whatever else looked toward being born and being true
        "Naas rammed up the ass
                    of every prophet before you
            licked away their delight in Daddy Cock

            Jesus Man Son don't let him snake his ways
                        through the bowels of your love
                tell everybody of FatherorMother
                            and Yahweh his lord
            then go on up
                    sit beside Elohim my father"

true to Baruch Jesus made the news

            which turned Naas rampant
                "that boy close his shit gate to me?
                        spread him on the cross
                            in front of me
            we'll see who's coming who's going"

on the withered tree of Naas Jesus abandoned Eden's body
                    going up to Good Dad
                last words : "woman, you have your son"
                    the child born of earth must die in her

Jesus gave his fire back to Cock Dad
and went to him to Priapos
who brought out whatever is before it was
fashioning out of his body from the shapes of his mind
that's why you see terminals of him in every temple
that everything that is born loves
his roadside stubs balance sweet fruit on their glans
for   he shepherded birth
                before earth womb bulged

when the swan nests on Leda
            that's Elohim buttering Israel
when the eagle rears up Ganymede
            Naas worms Adam
when the gold storms Danaë's snatch
            golden Elohim floors black Eden's tubes

and so through the stories of instruction
(when Heracles Mel-kart drove Geryon's cattle through Scythia
      he met
          . . . the snake woman in the desert
             . . . how the world was fathered
               . . . Naas bowing his head
                   clamps tail between teeth)

hear, sky
listen, earth
the Lord speaks
        fire of Elohim is inside
        Earth's windair the soul right alongside
Baruch is your Lord

Eden Israel married and divorced Elohim
        who said
      "Israel did not know me
         if she did
            that I am with Yahweh Straight Cock
    she would not have struck out in mother's ignorance
          at my fire in mankind"

the Lord has sworn and will not repent

so now take the Oath of Baruch

    "I swear by Goad Priapos who is above all
to guard these Secrets
and tell them to no one
I promise not to fall back
from Man Cock to Wom(b)man Cunt"

then you will see what *eye has not seen or ear heard*
                              what has not yet entered heart
and drink from *welling water springing up into everlasting life*
in the basin of the fountain of live bubbling water

                    for water has been taken from water
                              brack fish water below the arched sky
            swilling   in Eden's cunt
                the siren   allure ring   in her snaker tress
                          washes earth and animal men
                    fresh life water above the blue groined heaven
                          the light-flecked come of Cock Papa
          dyes pale bright the living
                    the fire sky lonely who ditched   their quimin

Elohim washes here
                    and having washed *did not repent*

go take a wife of whoredoms
for earth has done great whoredoms
departing from the Lord

Eden empties Elohim
                    that is the whole Secret
                    now watch out for
                              Serpent Naas
                    don't let him get
                              behind you

Elemental Creation

III. DIVIDING

Autonomic and Aliyan Texts

B. ALIYAN TEXTS

Enuma eliš

Akkadian text with other Semitic styles and attitudes, c. 1500 B.C. Texts: Labat, *Le poème babylonien de la création;* Lambert, *Enuma elish;* Landsberger and Wilson, "Tablet V of enuma eliš," *Journal for Near Eastern Studies* #20.

When sky above had no name
    earth beneath no given name

⎧APSU   the first   their seeder
⎨Deepwater
⎧TIAMAT
⎩Saltsea   their mother   who bore them
                                 mixed waters

Before pasture held together
      thicket be found
no gods being
no names for them
no plans

the gods were shaped inside them

LAḪMU AND LAḪAMU were brought out
                     named
while they grew
      became great
⎧ANŠAR and ⎧KIŠAR were shaped
⎩Skyline   ⎩Earthline   much greater

             made the days long
             added the years

⎧ANU was their son
⎨Sky   their rival
⎧ANŠAR made his first son ⎧ANU his equal
⎩Skyline   ⎩Sky

                  ⎰ANU   ⎰NUDIMMUD
and ⎱Sky   got⎨ Manmaker   equal
                            ⎩(EA)

⎧NUDIMMUD
⎨Manmaker
⎩(EA)   his fathers' boss
                            wide wise

                            full knowing
               ⎰ANŠAR   strong
stronger than ⎱Skyline his father
no equal among his brother gods

The godbrothers   together
stormed in ⎰TIAMAT
             ⎱Saltsea
stirred up ⎰TIAMAT 's guts
             ⎱Saltsea
rushing at the walls

     ⎰APSU
Not ⎱Deepwater hush their noise
⎰TIAMAT
⎱Saltsea struck dumb
They did bad things to her
     acted badly, childishly
     ⎰APSU
until ⎱Deepwater   seeder of great gods
                called up ⎰MUMMU
                          ⎱Speaker:
⎰MUMMU
⎱"Speaker   messenger   makes my liver happy
                       come!   ⎰TIAMAT
                       Let's go see⎱Saltsea."

They went   ⎰TIAMAT
     sat down in front of⎱Saltsea
     (talk about plans for their first-born gods):

⎧APSU
⎩Deepwater   opened his mouth   said
to ⎧TIAMAT   said loud:
   ⎩Saltsea
"The way they act makes me sick:
during the day   no rest
at night   no sleep

I'll destroy them!
    stop their doings!
It'll be quiet again   we can sleep"

      ⎧TIAMAT
When ⎩Saltsea   heard this
                she stormed
                  yelled at her husband
                  was sick
                  alone:

      "Wipe out what we made?!

      The way they act *is* a pain
               but let's wait"

⎧MUMMU   ⎧APSU
⎩Speaker answered   advising ⎩Deepwater: ⎧MUMMU
                           bad advice ⎩Speaker's
                                   ill-meant

"Go on!
      Put an end to their impertinence
                      then
rest   during the day
sleep   at night"

When ⎧APSU   heard him
     ⎩Deepwater   his face gleamed
                    for the hurts planned
                    against his godsons

hugged { MUMMU
      { Speaker
set him in his lap
kissed him

What they planned in conference was repeated
to their firstborn godsons
They wept
     milled around   distressed
     kept silence

{ EA
{ Waterhome   most understanding
                          skillful
                          wise
                          knowing all
                                  saw through the plot

    came up with a plan   made it up
crafted his spell   pure and mastering
made it sound the water
                   where slept { APSU
poured more sleep   { Deepwater well
stretched him out
soaked him with sleep

Counsel { MUMMU stuck still
      { Speaker

{ APSU
{ Deepwater's belt   crown   aura
 he   took off   tore away   ripped off
            tied up { APSU   killed him
                  { Deepwater
            tied up { MUMMU   shut him up
                  { Speaker

Found a house in {APSU
                 {Deepwater
led off {MUMMU by the nose
       {Speaker

After whipping his enemies   treading them
did {EA   rest   sureset victor
     {Waterhome
inside his holy home in deep peace

called it the Apsu
woven reed cult hut he founded

LAḪMU AND LAḪAMU
EA   and DAMKINNA
Waterhome and Earthandskylady   lived there
in greatness
in the shrine of fate
                 lodge of divine order

Wisest wise   {MARDUK   god was conceived
                      {Sunchild
                      {godsage
                          {MARDUK
in side the Apsu   {Sunchild born
in side godly Apsu   {MARDUK born
                          {Sunchild

{EA   his father   fathered him
{Waterhome
{DAMKINNA
{Earthandskylady   his mother   brought him out

goddess' tit he sucked
nurse nursed him full of fear

build seduced   raised eye flashed
manly at birth   mighty from the start

When ⎰EA   his father
      ⎱Waterhome who fathered him
                            saw him

he became happy
      laughed
                heart full of joy

He polished him up
    doubled his godness   raised above gods':

his lines   unknowable
                  fine-made
                  unthinkable
                  unseeable:
                  fourfold eye
                  fourfold ear

                  lips moved   fire flashed
                  fourfold   huge eared
                  samenumber eyes   saw all
                  highest god   tallest tall
                  hugest limbs   highest height

"My son   my son!
Sunchild   skySun!"

                                Dressed in 10 gods' aura
                                     strongest
                                     lightning charged

Then
⎰ANU
⎱Sky   bears the fourwinds
                          in front   the allwind the whirlwind
                                   made waves   ⎰TIAMAT
                                     stirring stirring the⎱Saltsea

      ⎰TIAMAT
The⎱Saltsea   troubled
                        comings and goings   day and night
                        the gods harassed again

the gods in their hearts plot evil
they   brothers   to ⌠TIAMAT
                      ⌡Saltsea:

"When they killed ⌠APSU
                    ⌡Deepwater your lover
    you did not go with him   but sat still

"Now *he*'s made the terror wind
        your belly's disturbed   *we* can't sleep

⌠"APSU
⌡ Deepwater be in your heart
⌠ MUMMU
⌡ Speaker   caught   you live   alone
                                    turn along
                                    don't love us

"Our eyes droop   burn
                    all the time
    We want sleep
    Fight!   and Revenge!
    Make them ghosts!"

⌠TIAMAT
⌡Saltsea   heard   brightened god
            said   "Advice you've given
                    Let's make stormmonsters
                                gods among them
                    All battle against gods!"

They troop to her
        surround ⌠TIAMAT
                  ⌡Saltsea
                            fiercely scheming   day and night
            raise the battle   growling roaring
                                forming fuming

Mother ⌠ḪUBUR
     ⌡undariver
     ⌊(TIAMAT)   all things molder

          makes weapons
            none like them

          bears dragons
            sharptoothed
            merciless fangs

          fills their bodies
            poison not blood

          clothes roaring dragons
            with dread
               splendor
          makes them gods

   (whoever sees them dies despairing
    once they rear up they never back down)

She raised up:

        a bašmu-dragon
        a mušḫuššu-snake
        a laḫamu-monster
        a Grand Lion
        a Mad Dog
        a Man-scorpion
        Howling winds
        a Man-fish
        a Bison

              They carry unstoppable arms
                are fearless
             her order so powerful
                  irresistible

She made 11 monsters   these
and from the gods   the firstborn
           surrounding her
              raised up ⌠KINGU
                        ⌡land from them all
            greatened him:

                  "ENUMA ELIŠ"   189

The first rank   the battle group leader
the arms raiser   the charger to war
the commander of the troops
she handed him   seating him in Council

"I've said the spell for you
        raised you in God Assembly
        filled your hand potent
                                over all the gods
    Rise! you my mate   my only
                        your name
                        over all the ⎰ANUNNAKI
                                    ⎱sky and earthgods"

She gave him the Tablets of Fate
                                hung them on his chest:
"So   your command not to be changed
        your word   fixed"

When ⎰KINGU   was over all
     ⎱land   was as ⎰ANU
                       ⎱Sky   he set the fates for his sons
                                        the gods:

"Words of your mouths douse the fire
  Mighty so in war
                shaking very Might"

COLOPHON TO TABLET I   *First tablet of enuma*
eliš written according to the original   *the tablet of Nabu-*
balat-su-iqbi   son of Na'id-Marduk   *by the hand of Nabu-*
balat-su-iqbi   son of Na'id-Marduk

COLOPHON TO ANOTHER VERSION OF TABLET I

Tablet I of enuma eliš after . . . a copy from Babylon writ-
ten according to the original   the tablet of Nabu-musetiq-
umi   son of . . .   who fears Marduk and Sarpanitum   and
did it not in fraud nor turning aside from the way . . . month
of Ayyar   9th day   27th year of Darius

When {TIAMAT / Saltsea}'d made her work strong
              raised her offspring to battle against the gods
              did evil to revenge {APSU / Deepwater}

It was told to {EA / Waterhome}
Hearing {EA / Waterhome}
              stilled in black quiet   wordless

When he'd thought   his anger ebbed
       he went up   to his father {ANŠAR who fathered him / Skyline}
         told what {TIAMAT / Saltsea} planned:

"My father {TIAMAT / Saltsea}   mothered us   hates us
                                calls a troop
                                mad   boils
all gods around her   those you made too   around her

They troop to her
      surround {TIAMAT / Saltsea}
                 fiercely scheming   day and night
       raise the battle   growling   roaring
                       forming   fuming

Mother ⌈ḪUBUR
       ⎰ undariver
       ⌊ (TIAMAT)   all things molder

                     makes weapons
                       none like them

                     bears dragons
                         sharptoothed
                           merciless fangs

                     fills their bodies
                       poison not blood

                     clothes roaring dragons
                     with dread
                         splendor
                   makes them gods

       (whoever sees them dies despairing
         once they rear up they never back down)

She raised up:
           a bašmu-dragon
           a mušḫuššu-snake
           a laḫamu-monster
           a Grand Lion
           a Mad Dog
           a Man-scorpion
           Howling winds
           a Man-fish
           a Bison

                   They carry unstoppable arms
                     are fearless
                 her order so powerful
                     irresistible

She made 11 monsters these
and from the gods   the firstborn
                 surrounding her

      raised up ⌈KINGU
             ⌊ land   from them all
      greatened him:

The first rank   the battle group leader
the arms raiser   the charger to war
the commander of the troops
she handed him   seating him in Council

'I've said the spell for you
        raised you in God Assembly
        filled your hand potent
                            over all the gods
Rise!   you my mate   my only
                        your name
                            over all the ⌠ANUNNAKI
                                         ⌡sky and earthgods'

She gave him the Tablets of Fate
                            hung them on his chest:
'So   your command   not to be changed
         your word   fixed'

When ⌠KINGU   was over all
     ⌡land   was as ⌠ANU
                      ⌡Sky   he set the fates for the gods his sons:
'Words of your mouths douse the fire
Mighty so in war
                shaking very Might' "

⌠ANŠAR   heard   how ⌠TIAMAT   stormed
⌡Skyline   ⌡Saltsea
         beat at his groin
         bit his lips
                    heart full of dread
                    spirit worried
         choked his cries:
                        ". . . to battle
                        You too must carry the arms you've made
You've killed   ⌠MUMMU   ⌠APSU
                  ⌡Speaker   ⌡Deepwater
         now ⌠KINGU
             ⌡land   marches before her"

{ NUDIMMUD
  Manmaker
  (EA)   answered . . . . .

      { ANŠAR   { ANU
So { Skyline to { Sky   his son   called

                      said this
                      full of wrath:

"Here is one powerful   my hero
  strength beyond   . . .
attack invincible   Go to { TIAMAT
                     { Saltsea   See her
so her anger be quieted
   her heart opened

If she will not heed your word
say it is our word   to still her"

When he'd heard his father's   { ANŠAR
                          { Skyline's order
he headed for her   along the way
                      but
when he saw the battle order of { TIAMAT
                          { Saltsea
he did not dare see her
  turned back to his father { ANŠAR
                      { Skyline
    cried what he had to say to   { TIAMAT
                          { Saltsea:

"My hand too weak
         to still you"

{ ANŠAR
{ Skyline   fell silent
          stared in the dirt

                              mumbling
                              head shaking

The ⌠ANUNNAKI   in Assembly   drew together
   ⌡sky and earthgods   lips sealed
                                   so silent stayed

                         No god would come at ⌠TIAMAT
                                              ⌡Saltsea
                         Facing ⌠TIAMAT
                                ⌡Saltsea none departs alive

The god ⌠ANŠAR   father of the gods
         ⌡Skyline   lifts himself   in splendor
                                       gathers his wits
                                       says to the ⌠ANUNNAKI
                                                   ⌡sky and earthgods

   "Whose strength is strong
                        will stand for his father
                        smash this war:

                                    ⌠MARDUK
                                    ⌡Sunchild   hero"

   So then ⌠EA   ⌠MARDUK
           ⌡Waterhome called ⌡Sunchild   to his place

   When he came he spoke his heart:

⌠"MARDUK
⌡ Sunchild   a plan   hear your father
   My son   ease my heart

   Go to ⌠ANŠAR
         ⌡Skyline   as to war   straight
   Stand right up!
   Say!
        Seeing you he will be at ease"

                              "ENUMA ELIŠ"   195

The ⌈bel
　　⎨lord
　　⌊(MARDUK) rejoiced at his father's word
　　　　　　drew near　　　stood at ⌈ANŠAR
　　　　　　　　　　　　　　　　　⌊Skyline

⌈ANŠAR
⌊Skyline looked on him　　his heart stuffed with joy
　　　　kissed his lips　　drove off fear

⌈"ANŠAR　　　not dumb
⌊ Skyline　　open your lips
　I bring you full heart
⌈ ANŠAR　　　not dumb
⌊ Skyline　　open your lips
　I bring you full heart

What man try you in battle?
A woman　⌈TIAMAT　　marches on you
　　　　　⌊Saltsea
My father　my maker　be happy　relax
Soon enough your feet on ⌈TIAMAT 's neck!
　　　　　　　　　　　　⌊Saltsea
My father　my maker　be happy　relax
Soon enough your feet on ⌈TIAMAT
　　　　　　　　　　　　⌊Saltsea's neck!"

"My son　　know all wisdom
still ⌈TIAMAT
　　　⌊Saltsea　　by your bright word!

Drive hard the storm car!

Not her helpers hold you back
drive them back!"

The ⌈bel　　　　rejoiced at his father's word
　　⎨lord　　　　heart bright
　　⌊(MARDUK)　said to his father:

196　　ORIGINS

{ "Bel   of the gods   Fate of the great gods
  lord
  (ANŠAR)
  if I be your avenger
     beat { TIAMAT
          Saltsea
     save your lives

               call Assembly
               make my fate all potent!
               Fate it!
                 in the { UPŠUKINNA   sit happy
                         Fates' hall
                 my word I set Fate like you
                 Unchangeable all I make
                 fixed   set   my lips command"

---

*COLOPHON TO TABLET II   Tablet II of enuma
eliš   after the text of the tablet . . . a copy from Assur*

---

*COLOPHON TO (another) TABLET II   Written
according to the original   the tablet of Nabu-aḫē-iddin
son of Eṭir-bel   son of the priest of Maš   no departure
from the way   no blame*

ANŠAR   opens his mouth
Skyline   says to KAKA   his speaker   these words:

"Speaker KAKA   cheers my heart
 I send you to LAḤMU and LAḤAMU

 You can make points   can chatter

 Bring the gods   my fathers   to me
        all the gods   come here together
                 talk with each other
                 sit at table
                 eat bread
                 drink wine

for ⌠MARDUK
   ⌡Sunchild   avenger fix fate

Go on KAKA   when before them   say them   I say:
⌠'ANŠAR   your son   sends me to you
⌡Skyline   commands me say his heart word:

⌠"TIAMAT   mothered us
⌡ Saltsea   hates us   calls a troop
                                     mad   boils
all gods around her   those you made too   around her
They troop to her
        surround ⌠TIAMAT
               ⌡Saltsea

                    fiercely scheming   day and night
        raise the battle   growling   roaring
                      forming   fuming

Mother ⌠ḪUBUR
        ⌡undariver   all things molder
        ⌊(TIAMAT)   makes weapons
                                     none like them
                        bears dragons
                              sharptoothed
                              merciless fangs
                      fills their bodies
                              poison not blood
                      clothes roaring dragons
                              with dread
                                  splendor
                    makes them gods

      (whoever sees them dies despairing
        once they rear up they never back down)

She raised up:
a bašmu-dragon
a mušḫuššu-snake
a laḫamu-monster
a Grand Lion
a Mad Dog
a Man-scorpion
Howling winds
a Man-fish
a Bison

They carry unstoppable arms
are fearless

Her order   ,so powerful
irresistible

She made 11 monsters   these
and from the gods   the firstborn   surrounding her
raised up   ⎰KINGU
⎱land   from them all
greatened him:
The first rank   the battle group leader
the arms raiser   the charger to war
the commander of the troops
she handed him   seating him in Council:

'I've said the spell for you
raised you in God Assembly
filled your hand potent
over all the gods

Rise   you my mate   my only
your name
over all the ⎰ANUNNAKI
⎱sky and earthgods'

She gave him the Tablets of Fate
hung them on his chest:

'So   your command   not to be changed
your word   fixed'

When ⎰KINGU   was over all
    ⎱land   was as ⎰ANU
                      ⎱Sky   he set the fates for the gods
                                                  his sons:

'Words of your mouths   douse the fire
 Mighty so in war
                    shaking very Might!'

I sent ⎰ANU
       ⎱Sky   could not face her
       ⎰NUDIMMUD
       ⎱Manmaker
       ⎱(EA)   feared   turned back

       ⎰MARDUK
       ⎱Sunchild   stood out   wisest wise   your son
                     made   to go face ⎰TIAMAT
                                    ⎱Saltsea

                   opens mouth   says to me:

'If I be your avenger
    beat ⎰TIAMAT
          ⎱Saltsea
    save your lives
                 call Assembly
                 make my fate all potent!
                 Fate it!

                        In ⎰UPŠUKINNA   sit happy
                          ⎱Fates' hall
                     my word   I set fate   like you
                     Unchangeable all I make
                     fixed   set   my lips' command'

Hurry here   fix him fast your fates
He will face your mighty enemy" ' "

Then KAKA left   made his way
                before LAḪMU and LAḪAMU the gods his fathers
                            fell down
                            kissed the ground at their feet
                            bowing deep
                            said to them:

⎰ "ANŠAR   your son   sends me to you
⎱ Skyline   commands me say his heart word:

⎰ 'TIAMAT   mothered us
⎱ Saltsea   hates us   calls a troop
                                         mad   boils
all gods around her   those you made too   around her
They troop to her
        surround ⎰ TIAMAT
                 ⎱ Saltsea
                            fiercely scheming   day and night
        raise the battle   growling   roaring
                                forming   fuming

Mother ⎡ ḪUBUR
       ⎨ undariver   all things molder
       ⎣ (TIAMAT)   makes weapons
                                none like them
                        bears dragons
                                    sharptoothed
                                    merciless fangs
                        fills their bodies
                                    poison not blood
                        clothes roaring dragons
                                with dread
                                        splendor
                        makes them gods

            (whoever sees them dies despairing
            once they rear up they never back down)

She raised up:
                a bašmu-dragon

a mušḫuššu-snake
a laḫamu-monster
a Grand Lion
a Mad Dog
a Man-scorpion
Howling winds
a Man-fish
a Bison

              They carry unstoppable arms
                   are fearless

            Her order   so powerful
                        irresistible

She made 11 monsters   these
   and from the gods   the firstborn   surrounding her
               raised up   KINGU
                     land   from them all
             greatened him:
the first rank   the battle group leader
the arms raiser   the charger to war
the commander of the troops
she handed him   seating him in Council:

"I've said the spell for you
      raised you in God Assembly
      filled your hand potent
               over all the gods

Rise!   you my mate   my only
                 your name
                    over all the ⎰ANUNNAKI
                             ⎱sky and earthgods"

She gave him the Tablets of Fate
                hung them on his chest:

"So   your command   not to be changed
       your word   fixed"

When KINGU was over all
   land was as ⌠ANU
         ⌡Sky
  he set the fates for the gods his sons:
"Words of your mouths douse the fire
 Mighty so in war
        shaking very Might!"

I sent ⌠ANU
   ⌡Sky could not face her
   ⌠NUDIMMUD
   ⎨Manmaker
   ⌡(EA)   feared turned back
   ⌠MARDUK
   ⌡Sunchild stood out wisest wise your son
       made to go face ⌠TIAMAT
            ⌡Saltsea

     opens mouth says to me:
"If I be your avenger
   beat ⌠TIAMAT
     ⌡Saltsea
   save your lives

          call Assembly
          make my fate all potent
          Fate it!

       In ⌠UPŠUKINNA sit happy
         ⌡Fates' hall
       my word I set fate like you
       Unchangeable all I make
       fixed set my lips' command"
Hurry here fix him fast your fates
He will face your mighty enemy' "

When LAḪMU and LAḪAMU heard shrieked
 ⌠IGIGI
 ⌡heavenly gods all   cried hard:
"What has come change she make this so!?
 We we don't know ways of ⌠TIAMAT
            ⌡Saltsea"

Then they gather   go
all great gods   fate fixers

                  come in to ⎰ANŠAR
                           ⎱Skyline

                  fill the ⎰UPŠUKINNA
                       ⎱Fates' hall

                  kiss each other
                  hold Assembly
                  talk to each other
                  seat for feast
                  eat bread
                  drink wine
                  pour sweet wine in their cups
  drinking tubes
          wet with liquor
                    bodies heavy
                drink drink
                    sweet heaviness through them
                fix fate for ⎰MARDUK
                         ⎱Sunchild their avenger

TABLET III ENDS

---

                make him a great throne
He sits in face his fathers   for speaking:

"You sure most heavy honor   among great gods
  your fate unequal
  your word   ⎰ANU
                  ⎱Sky

⎰MARDUK
⎱Sunchild   most heavy honor   among great gods
  your fate unequal
  your word   ⎰ANU
                  ⎱Sky

From now your word   unchangeable
     in your hand   lifting   lowering
                      unshaking
        your word
        your word   firm

No god cross your bounds

Support need god chambers
their sure chambers   your chamber

⎰ MARDUK
⎱ Sunchild   our avenger
we give you reign   over all
Take place in Assembly
your word   here   rule
your weapons   invincible
                    wreck your enemies

⎡ BEL
⎨ Lord
⎣ (MARDUK)   Live your faithful!
                 Die the god plots you ill!"

They extend a piece of cloth
     say to ⎰ MARDUK
          ⎱ Sunchild   their firstborn:

⎰ "BEL
⎱ Lord   your word first among gods
            'Make'   'Unmake'   so it is

    Open your mouth   cloth undone
    Say again   cloth whole"

Word from his mouth   cloth undone
Again his word   cloth formed

When gods   his fathers see his word
                   rejoice
                   say homage:

$$\begin{cases} \text{``MARDUK} \qquad \text{King!''} \\ \text{Sunchild} \end{cases}$$

They give him then   scepter   throne   and ball
                  invincible weapons   foe undoers

"Go!   Cut the breath of $\begin{cases} \text{TIAMAT} \\ \text{Saltsea!} \end{cases}$
   The winds carry her blood to unknown lands!"

The gods   his fathers   setting fate for $\begin{cases} \text{BEL} \\ \text{Lord} \\ (\text{MARDUK}) \end{cases}$

              clear him way
                   to full success

He makes a bow   calls it his weapon
    attaches the arrow
    fixes its cord

    picks a toothed-sickle   (holds it in his right hand)

    hangs the bow and quiver by his side

    sets it lightning in his face
    fills his body aflame

    makes a net   to catch $\begin{cases} \text{TIAMAT} \\ \text{Saltsea} \end{cases}$

    sets the fourwinds to hold her all
       the Southwind
       the Northwind
       the Eastwind
       the Westwind
    puts the net
       $\begin{cases} \text{ANU} \\ \text{Sky} \end{cases}$ his father   gave
                         by his side

    makes:
       the Evilwind   Imḫullu
       the Stormwind
       the dust storm

                    the fourwind
                    the sevenwind
                    the wreckingwind
                    the peerlesswind

The winds he makes   he looses all 7
to stir ⌠TIAMAT
        ⌡Saltsea's guts   they rush at his back

The ⌠bel
    ⌡(MARDUK)   then raises   the Hurricane
                                            his great arm
                        mounts   his storm car
                                            peerless   terrible
                        yokes   a fouryoke ' up
                                   the Destroyer
                                   the Ruthless
                                   the Crusher
                                   the Quick
                                            sharp toothed
                                            poisonous
                                            destruction familiar
                                            wrecking learned

Smiter   feared in battle   on his right
Combat   turns back the earnest   on his left
    clad   armorclad   in terror clad
horrible splendor covers his head

and the ⌠bel   went fast
        ⌡lord   along his way

and to ⌠TIAMAT   in her anger
       ⌡Saltsea   set his face
                                 holds in his lips a spell
                                 in his hands a plant against poison

This then his fathers race 'round him
          the gods   race 'round him
The gods his fathers race 'round him
          the gods   race 'round him

The bel   comes up
    lord   sees in side ⌠TIAMAT
                                ⌡Saltsea   the forces of ⌠KINGU
                                                          ⌡land
                                                            her lover
              sees them   his way upset
                                mind confused
                                acts chaotic

The gods   his aids   march at his side
                            see the brave   the foremost
                            lose sight

⌠TIAMAT
⌡Saltsea   casts up her word   turns not her neck
  savage   lips   rebellion:

"How honored you are   ⌠BEL
                         ⌡Lord   of the gods
    They come with you
        leave their place
        come to yours"

The ⌠bel
    ⌡lord   rears the Hurricane   his mighty arm
to ⌠TIAMAT
   ⌡Saltsea   enraged   raises his word:

"So   you are supreme   superb
            make your own heart make war
                                sons hate fathers
        you spurn motherlove
            make ⌠KINGU
                 ⌡land   lover
            make him   ⌠ ANU
                            ⌡ Sky   He is not
            plot ill for ⌠ANŠAR
                         ⌡Skyline   godking
            set evil against the gods   my fathers

208   ORIGINS

Let your men stand in arms!
You be armed
Come on!   You meet me in duel!"

⌈TIAMAT
⌊Saltsea   hears these words
                goes berserk
                loses sense
                cries madly   in piercing voice
                                       legs tremble both   full length
                calls a spell
                throws a curse

            Gods at war   sharpen arms

Come together   ⌈TIAMAT and ⌈MARDUK
                     ⌊Saltsea   ⌊Sunchild   wisest wise
raise at each other
join for battle

The ⌈bel
     ⌊lord   casts his net
                catches her
                looses Imḫullu   in her face   from behind him

⌈TIAMAT
⌊Saltsea   opens her mouth   gobble him
He   sends in Imḫullu   she'll never close her lips

The furywinds puff her belly to heartache
                              her mouth gapes
He flies the arrow   it rips her belly
                              tears her gut
                              splits her heart

He binds her
    cuts her breath
    throws her body down
    stands up   on her

⎧TIAMAT
⎨Saltsea   killed   who marched first
Her troops scatter
    gang breaks up
      the gods her aids who marched alongside her
                                shake fear
                                turn backs to keep
                                         save
                                            their lives

Circled   they cannot run
⎧MARDUK   binds them
⎨Sunchild   breaks their weapons

Thrown in nets   ensnared
        in caves   wailing
His punishment they carry   imprisoned   fettered

The Eleven   ⎧TIAMAT
               ⎨Saltsea   puffed full of horror
the Demontroop   marched at her face
he threw   in chains bound
their enmity   he crushed underfoot

⎧KINGU
⎨land   who was most strong
he bound   gave to ⎧UGGU
                     ⎨deathgod
    took off the Tablets of Fate
                        not *his* by right

                        sealed them with his seal
                        hung them on his chest

When he'd bound his enemy
          beat him
          dragged down the haughty foe
          completed the triumph of ⎧ANŠAR
                                    ⎨Skyline

When $\begin{cases}\text{MARDUK} \\ \text{Sunchild}\end{cases}$ had done   the will of $\begin{cases}\text{NUDIMMUD} \\ \text{Manmaker} \\ (\text{EA})\end{cases}$

made sure the captured gods
turned again to beaten $\begin{cases}\text{TIAMAT} \\ \text{Saltsea}\end{cases}$

stood her on her legs
split her head
cut her vessels

The Northwind   took off her blood   to Nowheres

His fathers see
     rejoice
     shout joy
     bring *him* gifts   homage

The $\begin{cases}\text{bel} \\ \text{lord}\end{cases}$ paused
     looked on her corpse

     splits the monster

     makes a fine thing:

     cleaves her like a clam
     puts up half for skies
     bars it separate   sets guards
         to keep her waters

Made way through heavens   looking there
    to make an Apsu   a dwelling for $\begin{cases}\text{NUDIMMUD} \\ \text{Manmaker} \\ (\text{EA})\end{cases}$

measured it
set up a house after it
    the ⎰EŠARRA
       ⎱Worldhouse
    the greathouse
       ⎰EŠARRA
       ⎱Worldhouse   he made the sky
                     made at home:
                            ⎰ANU
                            ⎱Sky

                            ⎰ENLIL
                            ⎱Earthgod

                            ⎰EA
                            ⎱Waterhome

---

*COLOPHON TO TABLET IV   . . .   146 lines   Tablet
IV of enuma eliš incomplete   after a damaged tablet
written by Nabu-bel-su   son of Na'id-Marduk the smith
for his soul's life   for his house's life   he wrote it   put it
in the Ezida*

He made stands for the great gods
    set the stars   like them   in lumasu-constellations
    set the year   limited
           for every 12 months   3 stars
    marked the year marks
    made the stand of ⎰NEBIRU
                ⎱Crosser   to mark their limits
        that none may cross or err
    beside it set ⎰ENLIL   ⎰EA
               ⎱Earthgod ⎱Waterhome
        opened ports on either side
        fixed the left lock   and the right

In her belly set the height of heaven
        made ⌠NANNARU
           ⌡Newmoon   shine
        gave him night

        gave it the   night spangle
                          to make the days:

"Turn all   all months   the first
                unstopping
                     your crown
shine hours   show 6 days
                the seventh day   a half crown
          half moons   two halves equal

When join ⌠ŠAMŠU
        ⌡the Sun   at Earthsky
                    bleach   bit by bit
                    go back
             at the darkness   approach the ⌠ŠAMŠU
                            ⌡Sun   way
                again in opposition

Here see your sign   go its way
Come close to ⌠ŠAMŠU
          ⌡Sun   both rule
                no favor

           . . . .

He gave days to ⌠ŠAMŠU
             ⌡Sun
    set day and night bounds . . .

           . . . .

    gathered ⌠TIAMAT
          ⌡Saltsea's   foamspit
    made
    melded clouds   full water
                raise wind
                make coolrain

made wet spit steam   piles
he did
      his hand

piled   a   mountain   her head
opened spring   rushing river
loosed   through her eyes   ⎰Parata
                             ⎨curvewater
                              ⎱(Euphrates)

                              ⎰Idikla
                              ⎨current
                              ⎱(Tigris)

stopped her nostrils   held back water

piled mountains   her teats
dug sprays   channels

bent her tail up   bound to band
⎰APSU
⎨Deepwater   underfoot
      her crotch   forks sky up

now: sky   top
      earth   set

made the womb   of ⎰TIAMAT
                    ⎱Saltsea   run
pulled out his net
sky earth   limits set

Made his   godwork   done his god task
      made chapels   gave to ⎰EA
                             ⎱Waterhome

      took   from ⎰KINGU
                            ⎱land   Tablets of Fate

brought
gave   firstgift   gave ⌠ANU
                                  ⌡Sky

                                gods of broken weapons
                                          flight

shoved   bound   'fore fathers

⌠TIAMAT—built   eleven devils
⌡Saltsea   broken weapons   foot-irons

made likenesses   at Apsugate

"Here's a sign they won't forget!"

Gods   saw him there
        shone
        delighted
                  LAḪMU and LAḪAMU   all his fathers
⌠ANŠAR
⌡Skyline   came to him
          greeted him "King!"

⌠ANU   ⌠ENLIL   ⌠EA
⌡Sky   ⌡Earthgod ⌡Waterhome   give him gifts

⌠DAMKINNA   his mother   joys him with a gift
⌡Earthandskylady   shines his face with tribute sent

USMU   who brought her gift to hiddenplace
        he made Apsuwarden   chapelkeeper

⌠IGIGI   gathered
⌡heavenly gods   all bowed down

⌠ANUNNAKI   all many
⌡sky and earthgods   kissed his feet

All   all   came   honoring

       before him   bowing:

"This is the King"

. . . .

In kingly aura   lifts the sickle
holds it right hand

slings the bow
takes the scepter
        left hand

. . .   his net   all glows the Apsu

He sits
    on his throneseat   in the chair

The gods   the many { EA   { DAMKINNA
                    { Waterhome { Earthandskylady

open mouth
say to great gods { IGIGI
                    { heavenly gods:

"Before { MARDUK
        { Sunchild   our son
now   your king

Proclaim his name!"

They say together:
        { "LUGALDIMMERANKIA
        { Kingofthegodsofskyandearth   his name

Trust him only!"

When reign to { MARDUK
        { Sunchild   given
                gave him plan   peace and well-being:

"From now   you keep the homes

You word   we obey"

{ MARDUK   opens mouth
{ Sunchild   speaks
                     to gods
                     his fathers

           says:
"Above the Apsu   you live
like { EŠARRA
      { Worldhouse   I build for you
below the dirt I gather to build
I build a house   my pleasant home
inside   holy grounds
I raise   holy cells
   fix my reign

When you rise from Apsu for Assembly
      night's rest for all of you

When you come down from skies for Assembly
      night's rest for all of you

I name it { 'BAB-IL CITY
         { City at the Gods-gate

       homes of   the great gods'

I build it with craftmasters"

The gods   his fathers   heard his speech
              asked { MARDUK
                   { Sunchild   firstborn
                       how this would be:

"On all your hands build
           who will have your agency?
  Over the dirt your hands build
           who will hold your court?

In { BAB-IL   called in fortune
   { Godsgate   found our shrines   forever!

Let the rebel gods   serve us daily
        your agency   ours
        none else do our jobs"

. . . .

⎰MARDUK   joyed
⎱Sunchild   answered these góds

⎰TIAMAT
⎱Saltsea—killer
            opened mouth   nobly:

"I command them serve daily
                my agency in your hands"

Gods bow before him
      proclaim him
      say   to ⎰LUGALDIMMERANKIA
               ⎱Kingofthegodsofskyandearth:

"Before ⎰BEL
        ⎱Lord   was son
    Now   he is   our king
                            whose bright words is our life
                Lord of splendor   sickle   scepter
                                    all-skilled

    Let ⎰EA
        ⎱Waterhome   plan
                    We are the builders"

COLOPHON TO TABLET V   Fifth tablet of enuma
eliš   Palace of Assurbanipal   king of the universe
king of Assur

MARDUK hears the oath of the gods
Sunchild decides to build a fine work

opens his mouth to EA
Waterhome
tells   heart plan:

"I will heap up blood
make a bone mass
build up a humanbeing
call it amelu
man
I will make humanbeing   amelu
man
He will serve the gods
they will be eased
So I will finish godways
the same revered
in two groups"

EA
Waterhome   says to him these words
to ease the gods
tells this plan:

"Only one of their brothers   cut loose
put alone to death
to make mankind
Let the great gods Assemble here
Cut loose the guilty   they will live"

MARDUK Assembles   the great gods
Sunchild directs   nobly
gives orders

The gods   in place   hear him out
The Prince   says these words to the ANUNNAKI
sky and earthgods

"If you said truth before   swear now:

Who brought rebellion?
      made ⌈TIAMAT fight ?
         ⌊Saltsea
   led   the battle?

Turn him in that made rebellion

I'll bear him nemesis
   leave you in peace"

The ⌈IGIGI
     ⌊heavenly gods   great gods   say to him
                             him
                  ⌈LUGALDIMMERANKIA
                  ⌊Kingofthegodsofskyandearth
             godspeaker
             their ⌈Bel
                  ⌊lord:

"It's ⌈KINGU   brought rebellion
     ⌊land   made ⌈TIAMAT
                     ⌊Saltsea   fight
             led the battle"

They tied him
      brought face ⌈EA
                ⌊Waterhome
     laid on him his guilt
     cut his blood

⌈EA   makes humankind   from his blood
⌋Waterhome   sets   them   godservice
⌊(NUDIMMUD)   sets gods free

a work   that work   unknowable

                        crafty planned by ⌈MARDUK
                                   ⌊Sunchild

done by {NUDIMMUD / Manmaker}

{MARDUK / Sunchild}   king of gods   split the {ANUNNAKI / sky and earthgods}

all of them   above   and below

gave them to {ANU / Sky}   to see to his command:

5×60 in sky   gods to guard there

made   in the same way   the ways of earth

in sky and on earth put 600 gods

After {MARDUK / Sunchild}   king   made law for all the gods

set the laws for the {ANUNNAKI / sky and earthgods}

of the sky and earth

the {ANUNNAKI / sky and earthgods}   open their mouths

say to {MARDUK / Sunchild}   their lord:

"Now {bel / lord}   who sets us free

what can we do for you?

We build shrinehome   then   call it: see

'Room-to-rest-nights'   may we sleep there"

When {MARDUK / Sunchild}   heard their words

his face gleamed bright like the day:

"Like another {BAB-IL / Godsgate}   built as you want

bricks be made

call it:

{'PARAKKA' / Chapel} "

The {ANUNNAKI
   {sky and earthgods use tools
               one year long   make bricks

    second year comes and they raise {ESAGILA   head   high
                                   {Headraising   as Apsu deep

        build a ziggurat   high as Apsu
                pinnacle
        make a house   a rest   for:

           {MARDUK {ENLIL   {EA
           {Sunchild {Earthgod {Waterhome

In glory he sat before them
        looked up from the bottom to {ESAGILA   horns   top
                               {Headraising

When they had made the work of {ESAGILA
                          {Headraising
                      the {ANUNNAKI
                          {sky and earthgods
        made their own chambers

        gathered   all   at the {ESAGILA
                           {Headraising
        they had built for his rest

He set the gods   his fathers   down to feast:
    "This is {BAB-IL   your home
          {Godsgate   which you love

       Come be happy in this place
         make feast"

The great gods take their places
                sit to drink zarbabu
                      festal beer
            sit down to feast

           are happy inside
                make rites in glorious {ESAGILA
                            {Headraising

then
          fix laws and fates
              posts in heaven and on earth
                  for all the gods

The fifty great gods sit
the seven gods of fate

            make fate:

{ ENLIL
{ Earthgod   lifts   his bow   his weapon   (which he made)
           puts it in front of them

The gods   his fathers   see the net   he made
                      see   the bow   its crafty make
           his fathers praise the work he made

{ ANU
{ Sky   lifts it
          praises it in the Godassembly

          kisses the bow: "This is my daughter"
          names the bow names:

              Longwood first
              . . . .   second
              Star/bow   third   I make it shine in sky

Praise revenging son
over all   no equal
guard the black-headed   his makings
          mankind

                          who worship him forever
                          praise his ways
                          unforgetting

Let him make great foodgifts for his fathers

They keep the houses   support the offerings
      bring incense to be smelled   whisper prayer

          image on earth   what he makes in sky

Order the black-headed to worship
         subjects   remember their god
         obey the goddess   at his saying
         bring foodgifts for god and goddess
         support their gods   unfailing

         build up their lands
         build more shrines
         black-headed wait on their gods

For us he is god   by many names
We count his fifty names:

Whose acts are very splendid whose ways are splendid—
            { MARDUK
            { Sunchild
  { ANU
  { Sky his father called him coming out
    Who sets food and drink   full stables
    Who whips the enemy with his weapon abubu
                      Deluge
    Who saved the gods his fathers in their trouble

    Yes   truly   the Sun's child brightest god
    May the gods always walk in the bright shining of his light

    Who put godservice on the peoples he made
                       quickened
                          so we may rest

    Making   wrecking   saving: his command
    They will pray to him

       { MARUKKA
       { (MARDUK)
God who makes everything
Makes the { ANUNNAKI
       { sky and earthgods   happy-hearted
                         eases them

       { MARUTUKKU
       { (MARDUK)
Truly   saves the land
      keeps the people

   the people praise him

      { BARŠAKUŠU   ŠUTUNŠAKUŠE
      {   Thronekeep
Who lifts himself to rule the world
            greathearted   warmbreasted

      { LUGALDIMMERANKIA
      { Kingofthegodsofskyandearth
the name we called him in Godassembly
raising his mouth's word over the gods his fathers
Truly { bel
       { lord of all the gods of earth and sky
         whose order subdues the gods

      { NARI-LUGALDIMMERANKIA
      { President-Kingofthegodsofskyandearth
the name we have given him : Watcher of all the gods
Who in sky and on earth makes our seats safe   in trouble
           sets posts for the { IGIGI   and { ANUNNAKI
                    { earthgods   { skygods
His name makes the gods shake   shiver in their seats

$$\left\{\begin{array}{l}\text{ASARULUDU}\\\text{Judge}\end{array}\right.$$

the name his father $\left\{\begin{array}{l}\text{ANU}\\\text{Sky}\end{array}\right.$ named him

Truly   light of the gods   strong chief

who   like the $\left\{\begin{array}{l}\text{šedu and lamassu}\\\text{protector genies}\end{array}\right.$

protects the gods and land

who saved our homes in trouble   in raging duel

$\left\{\begin{array}{l}\text{ASARULUDU}\\\text{Judge}\end{array}\right.$ called too $\left\{\begin{array}{l}\text{NAMTILLAKU}\\\text{God of life}\end{array}\right.$

by all the 600 gods

Who rebuilds the lost gods   as his own creatures

The $\left\{\begin{array}{l}\text{bel}\\\text{lord}\end{array}\right.$ whose pure spell rebreathes the dead gods

Foe beater   Praise him

$\left\{\begin{array}{l}\text{ASARULUDU}\\\text{Judge}\end{array}\right.$ third called $\left\{\begin{array}{l}\text{NAMRU}\\\text{Oath}\end{array}\right.$

The Pure God Who Shines Our Way

$\left\{\begin{array}{l}\text{ANŠAR}\\\text{Skyline}\end{array}\right.$ LAḤMU   LAḤAMU   each called him three names

said them to the gods   their sons

"Each of us called three of his names.

You call his names like us"

They rejoice   hear their word

in the $\left\{\begin{array}{l}\text{UPŠUKINNA}\\\text{Fates' hall}\end{array}\right.$ fix decision:

"We will raise his name

brave son   revenger   protector"

and take their places in Godassembly to say fates

all together in holy place   fix his name

COLOPHON TO TABLET VI   *Sixth tablet of enuma*
eliš . . .

{ ASARU
{ Ruler
gives fertile fields   sets seeds
makes grain   herbs   sprouts the green

{ ASARUALIM
{ Heavy Ruler
honored in council house   first in counsel
the gods wait to him   when fearing

{ ASARUALIMNUNNA
{ High and Heavy Ruler
honored   light of his father   who fathered him
Who leads well commands of { ANU   { ENLIL   { EA
                             { Sky   { Earthgod   { Waterhome

    their provider   fixes them income
whose šukussu-field is abundant   swelling

{ TUTU
{ Starter
who restarts them
Make the shrines pure   for rest
Make the spell   gods   rest
If they get up angry   they go back

Truly   first in the Godassembly
none of them his equal

{ TUTU-ZIUKKINA
{ Starter- Godband Life
Life of the Band of Gods
Who made the bright heavens for the gods
    holds their ways together
    sets their courses

May he never be forgotten among the hordes
his works be remembered

{ TUTU third called { ZIKU
{ Starter   { Purelife
Pure Maker
Sweet breaths' god
{ bel
{ lord   hearing and giving
makes richness and plenty
assures   the teem
makes our lack   fullness
whose sweet breath we breathe   in distress
Proclaim   Uplift   Worship his fame

{ TUTU fourth called { AGAKU
{ Starter   { Purecrown
the people praise him
{ bel
{ lord of pure spell   rebreathes the dead
                          pities bound gods
                          lifts the gods' levied yoke
                          makes mankind to save them work
Making mercy   whose power is to breathe life

His words last   unforgotten
in black-headed mouths   his hands' making

{ TUTU fifth called { TUKU
{ Starter   { Pure Spellspeaker
their mouth speak his pure spell
whose pure spell undoes the evildoers

{ ŠAZU
{ Heartknower
knows the hearts of gods
sees their guts
The evildoer cannot escape him
who sets Godassembly   makes their hearts happy
bends the rebel   shades the gods
wipes out evil   saves the right
keeps wrong   and   right apart

228   ORIGINS

ŠAZU   second named ┌ZISI
Heartknower   └Lowlifter
quiets the rebel
            praise him
Takes away pain from the body of the gods   his fathers

ŠAZU   third named ┌SUḪRIM
Heartknower   └Foeloser
with arm   tears out the enemy
confuses their plots
winnows them in wind
erases the evil ones   shaking

Gods   praise him

ŠAZU called fourth ┌SUḪGURIM
Heartknower   └Foestamper
who sets court
        creates the gods   his fathers
destroys the enemy   smashes their children
confuses them
none left
Call his name
Say it everywhere

ŠAZU   called fifth ┌ZAḪRIM
Heartknower   └Foeruin
praise
destroys the enemy
hunts down evil
brought hunted gods home
His name go on forever

ŠAZU   sixth ┌ZAḪGURIM
Heartknower └Allfoeruin
give him all praise
destroys all the enemy in war

ENBILULU
Adad of Bab-il

He is the grower god
                    strong
who names them
sets roastgifts
makes pasture and waterhole sure in the land
opens wells   sets waters

ENBILULU   second EPADUN
Adad of Bab-il   Watercourser

praise him
who waters earth
washes sky and earth
sets planting
fixes land
          to plow
          to pasture

          dam and trench
          and furrow

ENBILULU   third ENBILULU-GUGAL
Adad of Bab-il   . . . -Greatness

washes gods' crops
praise him
bel
lord of plenty
     of richness
     of heavy crops
gives richness
makes the homes rich
gives millet
drives up barley

$$\left\{\begin{array}{l}\text{ENBILULU}\\\text{Adad of Bab-il}\end{array}\right. \left\{\begin{array}{l}\text{ḪEGAL}\\\text{Plenty}\end{array}\right.$$

piles up plenty for the people
rains rich over wide earth
fixes green

SIR.SIR

piled up a hill on $\left\{\begin{array}{l}\text{TIAMAT}\\\text{Saltsea}\end{array}\right.$

carved $\left\{\begin{array}{l}\text{TIAMAT}\\\text{Saltsea}\end{array}\right.$ with his weapon

guides the land   steady shepherd
his head:
       a field of grain
       field rows high
leaps the broad deep   in anger
crosses   a bridge walk   to duel

SIR.SIR   second   MALAḪ

his boat is $\left\{\begin{array}{l}\text{TIAMAT}\\\text{Saltsea}\end{array}\right.$

       he rides her

GIL . . .

keeps grain heaps   huge piles
pushes up barley   millet
gives the land seed

GILMA

makes high godhouse last
builds fastness

barrel hoop
goods giver

AGILMA

high
takes the wave crown
makes the clouds
makes the sky last

ZULUM

who gives out lands
gives sections   foodgifts

⎧ MUMMU
⎨ Speaker
⎩
builds sky and earth
orderer
makes sky and earth pure
                    or

ZULUMMAR

                    of strength unequal among gods

GIŠNUMUNAB

maker of all people
maker of the parts of the world
who disappeared ⎧ TIAMAT 's gods
                ⎨ Saltsea
                ⎩
made men of them

                ⎧ LUGALABDUBUR
                ⎨ Fatherking deepleader
                ⎩
wrecked what ⎧ TIAMAT
             ⎨ Saltsea plotted
             ⎩
caught her weapons
strong base   from top to bottom

                ⎧ PAPGALGUENNA
                ⎨ Firstgreat of all lords
                ⎩

prime of all lords
power prime
highest of his brothergods
    of all gods

        ⎰LUGALDURMAḪ
        ⎱Highhouse King
gods' tie
bel
lord of the ⎰DURMAḪ
        ⎱Highhouse
first in godhouse
highest god

       ARANUNNA

counsels ⎰EA
      ⎱Waterhome
who makes the gods his fathers
whose high ways no god can equal

      ⎰DUMUDUKU
      ⎱Dukuson
the ⎰DUKU doubles his pure home
   ⎱(temple) Pure Home
the ⎰LUGALDUKU
   ⎱Dukumaster   does not judge without him

      ⎰LUGALLANNA
      ⎱Skyhigh King
whose power   among gods   is highest
bel
lord ⎰ANU
     ⎱Sky   strength
who ⎰ANŠAR
    ⎱Skyline   called to greatness

{ LUGALUGGA
{ Deathking
took them off in battle depth
who has all knowing   wideseeing

{ IRKINGU
{ Kingudragger
who took off { KINGU
            { land   in battle depth
passes rule on all
makes kingship sure

{ KINMA
{ Guide
who leads all the gods
gives direction
gods shake fear at his name
      shake in storm

{ ESIZKUR
{ Prayerhouse
comes high in prayerhouse
gods set gifts before him
so he give them work
no making without him
maker of 4 black-headed
without him no god sets length of days

{ GIBIL
{ Reedfire
fire that makes the point sharp
makes crafty arms in { TIAMAT battle
                     { Saltsea
widewise
sureseeing
so deepheart
gods cannot see the bottom

$\left\{\begin{array}{l}\text{ADDU}\\\text{Stormwind}\end{array}\right.$

his name   covers the sky
his wind blowing good over earth
then his speech blow clouds away
leave food for the people beneath

$\left\{\begin{array}{l}\text{AŠARU}\\\text{Leader}\end{array}\right.$

who leads the gods of fate
he owns their fate

$\left\{\begin{array}{l}\text{NEBIRU}\\\text{Crossing}\end{array}\right.$

point of heaven-earth crossing
who cross must cross him
$\left\{\begin{array}{l}\text{NEBIRU}\\\text{Crossing star}\end{array}\right.$ bright in sky
controlling   spinning around him
"He halves $\left\{\begin{array}{l}\text{TIAMAT}\\\text{Saltsea}\end{array}\right.$

               Call him $\left\{\begin{array}{l}\text{NEBIRU}\\\text{Crossing}\end{array}\right.$ holds the middle
keeps the skies' starcourse
the gods are his sheep   he is their shepherd

$\left\{\begin{array}{l}\text{TIAMAT}\\\text{Saltsea}\end{array}\right.$ master

cuts her life short and tight
as long as mankind lives   till days grow old
let her fade away   and ever keep away"

$\left\{\begin{array}{l}\text{BEL MATATI}\\\text{Lord of Earth}\end{array}\right.$

Father $\left\{\begin{array}{l}\text{ENLIL}\\\text{Earthgod}\end{array}\right.$ calls him

because he made the distances and the hard ground

$\left\{\begin{array}{l}\text{EA}\\\text{Waterhome's heart was high}\end{array}\right.$ hearing the $\left\{\begin{array}{l}\text{IGIGI}\\\text{earth and sky gods}\\\qquad\text{call his names}\end{array}\right.$

"Whose names his fathers raise   I call my name: $\left\{\begin{array}{l}\text{EA}\\\text{Waterhome}\end{array}\right.$

He rules my rites
   does my order"

Calling him $\left\{\begin{array}{l}\text{"ḫanša"}\\\text{fifty}\end{array}\right.$ the great gods call him whose names are fifty

Keep his names   the guide explain them
the converse of wise and knowing
the father pass them to his son
herders of cow and sheep open ear to them
be happy with $\left\{\begin{array}{l}\text{MARDUK}\\\text{Sunchild}\end{array}\right.$ $\left\{\begin{array}{l}\text{ENLIL}\\\text{Earthgod}\end{array}\right.$ of gods
so the land abound   and he grow rich

(Marduk)   His word is set
          His order unchanging
          No god calls back the word of his mouth

          Where he looks his neck looks too
          No god dares his wrath
          Widewise
          Deephearted

. . .

COLOPHON TO TABLET VII . . .

BEROSOS, FROM THE *BABYLONIAN HISTORY*

A Greek text by Berosos, c. third century B.C., taken from a
Babylonian source, c. 1200 B.C. Text: Jacoby, ed., *Die Fragmente der Griechischen Historiker,* Vol. 1. ". . ." is used to
separate fragments.

Berosos says in the first book of his *Babylonian History*
that he lived during the time of Alexander the Great

that he had consulted the public records of Babylon
which had been carefully preserved for 150 myriad years

that these records contain the history
                              of heaven, earth, and sea
of the first birth of everything
of the kings and their deeds

. . .

in the first year
Oan/Ea came
from the Persian Gulf
fish body
but under the fish head
man's head
fish tail
but underneath
man's feet
speaking like a man
destroying the mind

you can see him still
in the temple

picture/costume/priest?

he spent the day with the people
he ate no food
gave them letters learning skill
how to start a city
write laws
mark the land
sowing reaping
everything

ever since they've found
nothing else useful

sun goes down
Oan went back to the sea
but he'll be back tomorrow

he lives in the ocean at night

then others came
same place
read about them in the Book of the Kings

Oan left his word behind
he talked about how the world was born
the first birth
and how people can live together

. . .

(Oan's word)

shadow and water
many born and living there

marvelous their holding their self-born form

men two wings
or four and double-faced

one body two heads maybe
both sexes
a man a woman?
or goat-footed goat-horned
or horse-footed

horse behind
man in front
hippocentaur
Jušparik
Siren

born and lived
bulls men-headed
dogs four-bodied fish-tailed
horses dog-headed horse-bodied fish-tailed

all kinds
plus swimmers creepers snakers
plus many more
you'd be surprised

they kept borrowing from each other

pictures of them
in Baal's Temple
Babylon

they all lived inside a woman
she was their mistress
Omorka/Um-ruk
in Chaldean Thalath/Tiamat
in Greek Thalatta (sea)
equaling in number Selenĕ (Moon)

. . .

things were like that
when Baal-Marduk came rushing in
and cut the woman in half
the lower slice he made earth
the upper the sky . . .

Baal-Marduk cut off his head
the other gods mixed his blood with earth
and made figures/people
that's how we get minds
and share in gods' thoughts

BEROSOS, FROM THE "BABYLONIAN HISTORY"   239

. . .

Baal-Marduk
Greek Dios the light/Zeus
cut open the darkness (of the woman)
he sliced sky and earth apart
put everything where it belongs
(this the Greeks call cosmos)

everything that lived
that could not bear
the power of his light
checked out

. . .

Baal-Marduk
saw that the ground was lonely
that it did not live
he said to one of the gods
"cut off your head"
rubbed earth in the blood
made people and animals
who can bear his light air

. . .

Baal-Marduk
made the stars and the sun and the moon
and the five wandering stars

ABYDENOS, TWO FRAGMENTS

FROM THE *CHALDEAN HISTORY*

Fragments 1 and 4 from the Greek text by Abydenos, third century B.C., taken from sources in Mesopotamia, c. 1200 B.C. Text: Jacoby, ed., *Die Fragmente der Griechischen Historiker,* Vol. 1.

1.

first the sea: Tiamat

but Baal Marduk shrunk her up

built places for everyone from her
put a wall around Babylon
first city

when it was time
he left

4.

when Titan Adam swelled up out of the ground
huge and proud
better than the gods
he built a tower where Babylon is now

when it started to walk near the sun
[El's?] winds came and
blew it down

                              the wreck: Babylon
                            what we speak: Babble
                          though it had once been one

          Kronos El and Titan war

                   confusion of what had once been clear

                          meropes
                          "clear speakers"

          the Hebrews call confusion ⎰ "BABEL"
                                     ⎱ god's gate

THE DESCENT OF THE GODS

A Hittite text, c. 1400 B.C. Text: *Keilschrifturkunden aus Boghazkoi,* XXVIII, #4 and #5.

Gods   in the sky
                in the dark earth   listening:

                    Naras
                    Napsaras
                    Minkis
                    Amunkis

                    Ammezadus

                            the oldest gods

                        these gods' fathers
                                    mothers:

                    Anu
                    Antu
                    Isara

                    Ellila
                    Ninlila
                        now settled gods   strong.

In the sky Alalu was king
        then Anu   prime god   stood
            Alalu sat athrone
        and Anu   bowed
                put the cup to his hand

Alalu was king nine years long
Anu fought him in the ninth and beat him

Alalu fled in dark earth

Anu sat athrone in Alalu's place
Anu   athrone

Strong Kumarbi gave him food

              bowed
                    put the cup in his hand

In the sky Anu was king nine years long
Kumarbi fought him in the ninth

                              Anu   like Alalu

Anu faced Kumarbi's eyes   but could not

      fled his hands
                    a bird   loose in heaven
Kumarbi chasing
            catching feet
                  casting down Anu

                  biting balls off
                        gulping down
                                    sticking into stomach

      laughing   happy guts

Anu   looking back   speaking to Kumarbi:

            "Happy guts!   How be happy?
            A mighty weight grows inside:

            I fuck you with Stormer

            I fuck you with Tigris

Can you bear it?

I fuck you with Tasmisu.

Three horrible godseed.

At last   Kumarbi
                    smash your head on the rocks

                                    on your own mountain"

THE SONG OF ULIKUMMI

A Hurrian-Hittite text, c. 1400–1200 B.C. The language is
Indo-European with a Semitic admixture. Text: Güterbock,
The Song of Ulikummi.

Who   whose mind is wisdom   taking in   Kumarbi gods' father
I sing

Kumarbi takes wise thoughts into his mind:
                    he plans an evil day
                    he plots against the Stormgod
                    he plots a usurper
Kumarbi takes wise thoughts into his mind
                    strings them like beads

When Kumarbi had taken wise thoughts into his mind   he got up
from his chair right away   took a stick in his hand
                    put the winds for fast shoes beneath his feet
                    left his city Urkis
                    came into ikunta lulli   (Cold Pond?)

When Kumarbi came into ikunta lulli a rock lay there
                    Her length   three two-hour marches
                    her width   one two-hour march and a half

                    His mind pricked up at her under

                    he lay with the rock
                    his man-ness poured into her
                    He took her five times
                    He took her ten times

        (A hiatus of about forty lines. Impaluri, vizier to Sea, brings
        a message from Kumarbi)

"Kumarbi   says   'Kumarbi must always be   father of the gods' "

The Sea spoke to Impaluri   when he had heard his words:
"Impaluri   my vizier   hold your ear to my words
  the words I tell you   Go and tell these words   certainly
  to Kumarbi:

  Go now   and say to Kumarbi:
                        'Why do you come to my house   and leave
                        in anger?
                        Fear takes my house
                        fear takes the slaves

                        Cedar incense is broken for you
                        food already cooked for you
                        singers keep their lutes ready
                        for you   day and night

                        So   get up
                        come back to my house' "

Kumarbi did get up   Impaluri walked in front of him
Kumarbi left his house
Kumarbi made travel
Kumarbi went into the house of Sea

And Sea said:
                        "Set up a seat for Kumarbi to sit on
                        set a table for him
                        Bring him to eat and drink
                        bring him beer to drink"
The cooks brought things to eat
the cupbearers brought him sweet wine to drink

                        They drank one time
                        they drank two times
                        they drank three times
                        they drank four times
                        they drank five times
                        they drank six times
                        they drank seven times

              (More broken and lost lines)

. . . stone gave birth to stone . . .

The midwives brought out his birth
the goddesses of fate and the Mother-goddesses took the child
   put him on Kumarbi's knees
Kumarbi began to be happy about this son
  began to dandle him
  began to give him a best name
Kumarbi said to himself:

   "What name shall I set on him
   this son
   the goddesses of fate
   and the Mother-goddesses
   gave me?

   He leapt from her body like a blade

   let him go on
   and his name be Ulikummi

   He will go up to the skies to be king
   He will beat Kummiya the best town
   He will attack the Stormgod
    pound him like powder
    stomp him like an ant
    and break Tašmišu off like a reed
   He will toss all the gods down from the skies like birds
    break them like empty pots"

When Kumarbi had said these words he said on to himself:
   "Who will I give him to this child?
   Who will take him for a gift?
   Who will hide him
    keep him in the dark earth?
   So the Sungod in the sky will not see him
   or the Moongod
   So the Stormgod strong king of Kummiya
    will not see him
    will not kill him
   So Ištar queen of Nineve the woman
    will not see him
    will not break him off
     like a reed?"

Kumarbi said these words to Impaluri:
        "Impaluri   hold your ear to my words
                     the words I tell you
                     take a stick in your hand
                     put the winds for fast shoes
                     beneath your feet
                     go to the Irširragods
                     say these words   strong
                     to the Irširragods:

     'Come
             Kumarbi   gods'father calls you to gods'house
                 . . .
     Come right away' "

                              "the Irširragods
           will take him   the child
           carry him in the dark earth
           They will not let the greatgods see him"

When Impaluri heard the words
                        he took his stick in his hand
                         put the winds for fast shoes
                         beneath his feet
                     Impaluri went
                            came to the Irširragods
Impaluri said the words to the Irširragods:
        "Come
             Kumarbi   gods'father calls you
            You will not know why but hurry
                            Come"

When the Irširragods heard the words
                      they came right away
                  got up   and came
                  the whole way at once
                  came to Kumarbi

Kumarbi said to the Irširragods:

>"Take this child   for a gift   care for him
>take him into the dark earth
>Hurry   right away
>Set him up like a blade
>on Upelluri's right shoulder
>
>He'll grow a yard a day
>   a rod a month
>His stone growth will put out the eye"

When the Irširragods heard the words
        they took the child off Kumarbi's knees
    the Irširragods lifted up the child
                bound him to their chests like cloth
                lifted him up fast
                set him on Enlil's knees
    Enlil lifted his eyes
        saw the child before the god
        a body of slate

Enlil said to himself:
        "Who is this child
                        the goddesses of fate
                        the Mothergoddesses raise?
            who will see   the wars of the great gods
            This is an evil plan of only Kumarbi
            who sets up a usurper   of slate
            against the Stormgod he set up"

When Enlil finished speaking
                they put the child on Upelluri's right shoulder
                like a blade

The slate grew   strong waters made him grow
He grew a yard a day
            a rod a month
                    his stone growth put out the eye

When it came to the 15th day
                the stone had grown high
He knelt in the sea   yet like a blade he stood out
                    above the water
        the stone stood
               tall like a pillar
     The sea came up to his belt
     like a girdle

    He was lifted up like a tower
    reached the temples
    and the gods' chambers in the sky

The Sungod looked down from the sky
      saw Ulikummi
Ulikummi saw the Sungod

The Sungod said to himself:
      "What strong god stands in the sea there
      his body not like other gods'?"

The Sungod of the skies   his face changed
     he went down to the sea
     he put his hands to his head
     then lowered them to his sides
     gave up his own anger

When the Sungod of the skies saw the stone
he crossed the mountains for a second time that day
he left
  went to the Stormgod

Tašmišu said   seeing the Sungod coming:

     "Why is he coming
          the Sungod of the skies
          king of the earth?
    Why he comes   it must be heavy
    not to be dealt with lightly
    The war must be strong
    the struggle must be strong

    Upset in heaven   death and hunger for the earth"

The Stormgod said to Tašmišu:
>"Set up a seat for him to sit on
>set a table for him to eat on"

They spoke   the Sungod came to their house
They set up a seat for him to sit on
>>but he did not sit

They set a table for him to eat on
>>but he took nothing

They gave him   a cup
>>but he did not drink

The Stormgod said to the Sungod:
>>"Is the chamberlain bad
>>>who set up a chair
>>>>you did not sit in?
>>>Is the steward bad
>>>who set a table
>>>>you did not eat from?
>>>Is the cup-bearer bad
>>>who gave you a cup
>>>>you did not drink from?"

>(More lost material; the Sungod must have told what he saw,
>placating the Stormgod)

The Stormgod said to the Sungod of the skies:
>>"Bread on the table will be good
>>>Eat now
>>Wine in the cup will be good
>>>Drink now
>>Eat and be full
>>Drink and be full
>>then arise and go up to the skies"

The Sungod heard these words and was happy in himself
>>The bread on the table was good
>>>He ate
>>The wine in the cup was good
>>>He drank
>>Then the Sungod arose and went up to the skies

When the Sungod of the skies left
the Stormgod took wise thoughts into his mind
The Stormgod and Tašmišu clasped each other
                          left the temple   the chamber
His sister Ištar came from the skies   brave
        Ištar said to herself:

                "Where are the two brothers running?"
                            she set herself
                            stood up
                      in front of her two brothers

They clasped each other
      went up to Mount Ḫazzi

The king of Kummiya turned his face
                      set his eye on the horrible Slate
He stared at the horrible Slate
He was angry   then scared

The Stormgod sat down on the ground
his eyes spilled tears like streams
The Stormgod   eyes full of tears   said:

                "Who can bear it
                            the violence of this one?
                      Who can fight it?
                      Who can bear it
                            the fear of this one?"

Ištar said to the Stormgod:
                "My brother
                He knows nothing
                but he is tentimes brave
                      . . .
      (About thirty lines missing. Ištar seems to suggest herself as a
      fit adversary)

Ištar sang   set out a rock from the sea
A huge wave came up from the sea
The huge wave said to Ištar:

          "Who are you singing to?
            Who do you fill your mouth with song for?

          The man is deaf
                   hears not
          His eyes are blind
                   he does not see
          He is not merciful
          Go away Ištar
          Find your brother
          while Slate is not brave yet
          while his skull is not horrible yet"

When Ištar heard this
          she put out her fire
          threw away her harp and galgalturi
               and golden jewels

       . . .
     (She tells the Stormgod; he instructs Tašmišu)

     "Tell them to mix the fodder
          bring perfumed oil
          anoint the horns of Šerišu
          plate the tail of Tella with gold
    They must turn the axle and wheels
          put strong braces inside
and on the outside   for cover   heavy stone

    They must call out the thunder storms
    Rains   winds   breaking rocks for 90 miles
              swamping rocks for 800 miles
    They must call the rains   and the winds
    They must bring the lightning
                sharp-flashing
       out from the sleep-chamber
    They must bring out the carts
    Set them up now
    then report to me"

When Tašmišu heard the words   he hurried   raced
                    brought Šerišu from pasture
                    brought Tella from Mount Imgarra

                    Hitched them on the front porch
                    brought perfumed oil
                    anointed the horns of Šerišu
                    plated the tail of Tella with gold
                    turned the axle and wheels
                    put strong braces inside
                    covered the outside heavy stone
                    and called out the thunder storms
                                rains and winds
                    which break rocks for 90 miles

                . . .

            (About thirty lines lost)

He took a stand to fight
He took up his weapons
He took the wagons
    brought the clouds from the skies

The Stormgod set his face at Slate
                stared at him:
                      His height . . .

          (About fifty missing lines. The preliminaries of the battle
          are staged; are indecisive)

The gods heard the call
        took their places in the wagons
Aštabi leapt into his cart like a. . .
        arranged the carts   (Aštabi=
Aštabi thundered   Zababu=
                in thunder went down to the sea   Ninurta)

. . .

Slate shook the skies
                 flapped the skies like an empty cloth
Slate grew high
Slate was on the earth   reached 1900 miles
                                up into the skies
                                reached the temple
                                and the gods'house
He was 9000 miles tall
          9000 miles wide
He overtopped the gate of Kummiya like a . . .
Slate rose over Ḫebat and the temple
Ḫebat heard no news of the gods
          could not see the Stormgod or Šuwaliyatta with her eyes
                                            (Šuwaliyatta=
                                            Nergal)

Ḫebat said to Takiti:
                 "I can't hear the Stormgod's word
                 I hear no news of Šuwaliyatta
                 and all the gods
                 Has this slate man Ulikummi beaten
                 my husband
                 the heavy Stormgod?"

Ḫebat said again to Takiti:
                 "Hear me
                 Take a stick in your hand
                 Put the winds   fast shoes
                 beneath your feet

                 . . . go
                 Maybe the Slateman has killed him
                                killed my husband
                                the heavy
                                Stormgod
          Report back to me"

          (About fifty lines broken and lost. Takiti fails)

When Tašmišu heard the Stormgod's words
he got up right away
    takes a stick in his hand
    puts the winds   fast shoes   beneath his feet
    went up to the high tower
    stood across from Hebat   said:

        "The Stormgod has told me to go to a low place
until he fills the years fixed for him"

When Hebat saw Tašmišu   she almost fell off the roof
She would have fallen by one step   but the women of the palace
    held her   stopped her from falling

When Tašmišu finished speaking   he went down from the tower
                        went back to the Stormgod
Tašmišu said to the Stormgod:

        "Where shall we sit down?
        On Mount Kandurna now?
        If we sit on Kandurna
        another will sit on Mount Lalapaduwa
        If we do not
        there will be no king   in the skies above"

Tašmišu said again to the Stormgod:
        "Come
            Let us go to the Apsu   see Ea
            ask for the fatetablets

        When we come to the gate of Ea's home
            we bow by the outer door 5 times
                by the inner door 5 times
                15 times when we come before Ea
        Maybe Ea will hear us
            have mercy on us
            give us back our reign"

The Stormgod hurried when he heard Tašmišu's words
    got up from his seat right away
The Stormgod and Tašmišu clasped each other
        went the whole way at once
        came to Apsu

The Stormgod came to Ea's house
        bowed 5 times by Ea's outer door
        bowed 5 times by Ea's inner door
When they came before Ea
      he bowed 15 times

             (Great fragmentation and loss. The Stormgod
             and Tašmišu enlist the aid of Ea)

Ea said to Enlil:
       "Don't you know Enlil?
       Has no word come to you?
       Don't you know him:
             the usurper Kumarbi shaped
                 against the Stormgod
             the Slate-man who grew up
                 in the water
             9000 miles tall
                 like a tower raised?"

          (More lost lines. Ea goes on to Upelluri)

When Ea finished what he had to say
he went to Upelluri

Upelluri raised his eyes
          saw Ea
Upelluri said to Ea:
       "Long live Ea"   and stood
Ea prayed life to Upelluri
          "Long live Upelluri on the dark earth
           the skies and earth rest on him"

Ea said to Upelluri:
       "Don't you know Upelluri?
       Has no word come to you?
       Don't you know him:
             the usurper Kumarbi shaped
                 against the Stormgod
             the Slate-man who grew up
                 in the water
             9000 miles tall
                 like a tower raised?

He has swamped the skies
the temples
Ḫebat
Are you so far away from the dark earth
Upelluri
you don't know this hard god?"

Upelluri said to Ea:
"When they built the skies and the earth on top of me
I was not aware
And when they came and cut the skies from the earth
with a slicer
Again I was not aware
Now my right shoulder something hurts
but I don't know who the god is"

Ea heard the words
turned Upelluri's right shoulder
The Slate-man stood
on Upelluri's right shoulder
like a blade

Ea said to the Old gods:
"Hear my words   Old gods
who know the old words

Open the storehouses of old
of father time   of grandfather

Bring the seal   old   of fathers
then seal again

Bring out the first slicer
which cut skies from earth

This Slate-man   Ulikummi
Kumarbi brought up as a usurper
against the gods
we will cut beneath his feet"

Tašmišu   on his knees   to Ea
                       said:
          "He has changed . . .
          I see the dead
          all over the dark earth
          They are dust fallen
          the evil stands"

Ea said to Tašmišu:
          "I have already hit the Slate-man
          Ulikummi
          Now   go   and you fight him   second

          The Slate-man stands like a blade
                    no more"

Tašmišu was happy
          called 3 times
          called into the skies

          The gods heard

          called 2 times

          The Stormgod   strong king of Kummiya heard

They came to Assembly
          all the gods
                   roared bull-roars
                             against
                             the Slate-man
                             Ulikummi

The Stormgod vaulted into his wagon like a . . .
          went down to the sea in thunder
          gave battle to the Slate-man   the Stormgod

The Slate-man said to the Stormgod:

          "I tell you what   Stormgod
             you beat against yourself

I tell you what   Stormgod
    you only beat against yourself
Kumarbi has a plan
    like beads on a string   in his mind
I will go up into the skies
    to be king
I will beat Kummiya   the best town
      the temple
      the chamber
and toss the gods down from the skies
    like birds

   . . .

(The rest is lost. Kumarbi-Ulikummi must have lost)

ILLUYANKA

A Hittite (Anatolian) text, c. 1350 B.C., under Mesopotamian influence; a text for recital during the Purulli (New Year) Festival. Text: Laroche, *Textes mythologiques hittites en transcription*.

The words for Kella, priest of the Stormgod of Nerik.
The cultus tale for the Purulli Festival of the Stormgod of the Skies;
no longer in use:

The land be fruitful and abundant. The land be guarded;
so when it is fruitful and abundant, keep the Purulli Festival.

The Stormgod ⌠ IM ⌡ (Tešub) and Illuyanka the Dragon fight in
Kiškilušša; the Dragon Illuyanka beats the Stormgod.
The Stormgod calls on all the gods:
"Come help me."
The goddess Inara makes a feast:

        She fixed up a lot of everything—

           vats of wine
           vats of marnuwan liquor
           vats of walḫi liquor

           full and many

                    then went to Zigarata.
She ran into Ḫupašiya, a man. Inara said,
"Look, Ḫupašiya, I want to do this and that. I want you to help me."
Ḫupašiya said to Inara, "O.K. If I can fuck you, I'll go along
and do what you want."
So he fucked her.
Then Inara brought Ḫupašiya home and hid him.
Inara put on her best things and vamped the Dragon Illuyanka
up from his hole: "Look. I'm having a feast.
Come eat and drink."

The Dragon Illuyanka came up with his boys. They ate and drank.
They drank up all the vats, then were full. So they couldn't go
back down into their hole.
Ḫupašiya came and tied up the Dragon Illuyanka with a rope.
The Stormgod came and killed the Dragon Illuyanka.
The gods supported him.
Then Inara built herself a house on a cliff near Tarukka.
She settled Ḫupašiya in the house.
She said to him: "When I go away don't you look out
the window; you might see your wife and kids."
Twenty days passed and the man opened the window and saw his
wife and children. When Inara came home, he cried, "Let me go home!"
Inara said to Ḫupašiya, "You won't be opening any more windows!"
She killed him, fighting, and the Stormgod spread sahlu-weed on
the ruined house. The man died unhappy.
Inara came back to Kiškilušša, and gave her house to the king.
So the king owns Inara's house.

This is how the story was told later:

The Dragon Illuyanka beat the Stormgod, took heart and eyes from
him. The Stormgod wanted revenge.
He took a slave's daughter to be his wife. He fathered a son.
When the son grew up he married the daughter of the Dragon
Illuyanka.
The Stormgod tells his son:

> "When you go to your wife's house ask for heart and eyes."

When he got there he asked for heart and they gave it to him.
Then he asked for eyes and they gave him. He carried them back
to the Stormgod, his father. So the Stormgod got his eyes and heart
back.

When the Stormgod's body was back in shape, he went to the sea
to fight.

He fought the Dragon Illuyanka   and almost beat him. But the son
of the Stormgod, who was with Illuyanka, called into the skies
to his father:

"I'm with him.
Take me with him!"

So the Stormgod killed the Dragon Illuyanka and his son too,
and revenged himself on Illuyanka.

FROM HESIOD, *THEOGONY*
(ZEUS AND TYPHOON)

This Greek tale of Zeus and Typhoon is from Hurrian-Hittite and earlier Indo-European traditions. The Greek text dates from c. 600 B.C.; the Indo-European forerunners, from before 2300 B.C. Text: Hesiod's *Theogony* (West, ed.).

Zeus stuffing chalkmen Strainers into dead wombs underground Finish

Typhoon last son of monster Earth from father Pit the Death
                    through golden Love
            in his hands held strong acts
                    his feet of gods never hurting never rest
shoulders hunching a hundred heads each a dragon snake of fear
                    that flick dank dusky tongues
            his eyes gouting flame peeled look out
                        from god-mock heads
in each astounding face a voice a wordnoise no other god re-makes
                    stately Typhoon spoke
        god-tongue bull-bellow lion-waul shaking his unguarded heart
                    dog-whelp (that's hard to swallow)
whistle streaking through air that made mountains back his tunes
                    this day something might have happened
            no one could make up: Typhoon new king of gods and men
                        if old king Zeus
hadn't had sharp eyes slithery mind
                        cracked untired thunder so stiffly
            earth sky sideless sea Ocean rivers pit wombs below
                        echoed threw it back
when her king rose up in war his deathless feet shook Olympos
                Earth wailed
            Zeus ranting his thunder lash
                        Typhoon screaming fire
flared into sunheat that checked the violet sea
                    they filled the wind then snapped it away
            turned earth sea sky to ceaseless restless
                    foam scum

soared up shake waves that combed foreshores headlands
                    inside and around
         slapped Earth with timeless hands
                        so she couldn't stop heaving
ran fear into Hades unseen king of those who wait and rot
      into the Strainers circling Kronos beneath Pitdeath
        who hid from their cries that swept tides
              from their fight with death in the other
Zeus hoisted his strength strapped on lightning thunder
                            sparkling flash
                leapt from Olympos
      struck
                    roared off
every godword head
                from wonderful
      Typhoon
                  who
lady-tamed
              cut-whipped
      by the bundled
                voltage sticks
thrown
      tumbled
            head down
                until he sprawled
      a slag heap
on his mother's lap
            monster Earth
              cried
      storm-broken
            king Typhoon
      flickered fire
                in secret forests
      on the jagged mountain
           where he'd been sheared
flaring godword breath
      he burned monster Earth
           like the lead

                    smelters cook in groundpit holes
       like iron strongest metal
                              fire lady-bends
                                    in hill forests
                 molten on goddess Earth
                           in palms of Hephaistos
                                    his breath
                           roaring blaze
                                    softened
                           made her run
in his heart
              Zeus cried
                           threw Typhoon
              into father
                           broad Deathpit

Typhoon's children are the winds of strong water
                           except the North and South
              and West who clears off clouds
         gods bring these to help us before we die
no telling when typhoons will blow
                        random fitful flaws panting on the sea
              trouble when they fall on Ocean
                              when he is misty dark
their pitdeath breath scatters ships sinks sailors
                        helpless whoever they catch
              in flower time they rip up boundless Earth
                              murder the acts of love
people born to earth commit on her
                        stopping them
              with dust with difficult voice

FROM APOLLODORUS, THE *LIBRARY*
(ZEUS AND TYPHON)

This Greek tale of Zeus and Typhon by Apollodorus, c. third century B.C.–first century A.D., is drawn from a pre-Hesiodic source in Greek, which in turn comes from earlier Indo-European sources. Text: Apollodorus, *Bibliotheca* (Frazer, ed.).

1.

                the gods Old Thunderers destroyed
        the giants angry Earth
in anger
                fucked Tartarus
        did let him father Typhon on her
cave-birth
                between man & beast
        his size & strength were
greater than Earth's other children
                human to thighs bulked
        large above all
mountains
                whose head for largeness
        brushed the stars
his hands reached east & west
                projected
        a hundred dragons' heads
down from the thighs snakes
                coiled pulled erect
        to reach his head
were hissing feathers
                on his body
        wild hair flew out in
wind from head
                to cheeks 't was
        like fire in his eye

                    so tall
                              old Typhon was
                hurled burning rocks
was screeching
                              hissing
                spouted a jet of fire from
his mouth
                              en route to heaven

2.

                              careening toward sky was Typhon
                sighted by gods
escaped him
                              made for Egypt
                there they would change to
animals
                              one left behind
                Old Zeus Bright Sky
far off could volley
                              thunderbolts
                would close in flatten him with adamantine
sickle
                              there goes monster-
                man he's almost
in Syria 's got old Zeus
                              pursuing (sez)
                "he's wounded"
wrestles him now entangling
                              himself in Typhon's
                coils entwined
who grasps the sickle
                              severs the sinews of
                his hands & feet
& hoisted on shoulders
                              through the sea he hauls

                the Thunderer back to
his cavern home
                          will drop him hide
               sinews in bearskin
sets a guard there
                         "Dragon Lady"
              "Dolphin"
"Virgin"
                          halfway created between
             man & beast

3.   ___   ___

                         in sequel
              Hermes Pillar God came
& Goat Pan
                          stole the sinews back
              made Zeus a perfect
fit (who saw it?)
                          's got his strength again
              Zeus
in a chariot of winged
                          horses riding down sky hurled
              thunder at Typhon
chased that monster to
                          Lame Mountain
              where the Fates would trick him
got him to taste
                          "ephemera"
              are fruits they said would
strengthen him
                          from there to Thrace again
              pursued battled around
the bloody hill tossed up whole
                          mountains Zeus thrust
              back at him by force of
thunderbolt

                    a stream of blood
              gushed from
        its rocks thereafter called
                    Blood Mountain

4.

                    in flight through
              the Sicilian Sea
        old Zeus threw Aetna on him
                    "that great mountain"
              to this day erupts with
        fire
                    thunderbolts
              touched off when thrown
        ages before

FROM OPPIAN, *HALIEUTICA*

This Greek text by Oppian, c. third century A.D., stems from
a pre-Hesiodic source in Greek, which in turn comes from
earlier Indo-European sources. Text: Oppian, *Halieutica*
(Mair, ed.).

savior of Zeus but Typhon's
slayer
tricked the old snake-
man with promises
banquets of fish
(he said)
would draw him from his
deep hole to the sea's
edge vulnerable
to their lightnings
crack-of-fire
thunderbolts that flattened him
blazed in that heat storm
beat his hundred heads on
rocks
carded like wool the yellow
dunes still red with Typhon's
blood o Hermes
counselor
god of fishermen
among old powers of
the hunt

THE BATTLE BETWEEN YAM AND BAAL

A Ugaritic (Canaanite) text, c. 1450 B.C. The Ugarites were a Semitic people of the north Syrian coast. Text: Gordon, *Ugaritic Textbook,* Text 68.

KOTHAR WA-KHASIS   (Smart & Slick)
says:
                    "Oh Prince BAAL   (Lord)
                    I told you once
                    I'll tell you again
                    Rokhab 'arafot: (Cloud Rider)

                    Your enemy Baal
                         Now
                    Your enemy
                         Now
                    Crush him!
                         Now
                    Destroy your troubler!

        You'll be king of the world   have your way forever"

Kothar lays out two clubs
    tells their names:
                    "Your name
                    you are
                    YAGRUŠ   (Chaser)

                    Chaser
                    chase YAM   (Sea)
        Chase Yam off his seat   NAHAR off his throne   (River)
        Whirl in Baal's hand   an eagle between his fingers
        Hammer Royal Yam
            Judge Nahar   in the back
                                   between his shoulders"

The club whirls   in Baal's hand
            an eagle   between his fingers
        hammers   the back of Royal Yam
                                 between the shoulders
                                 of Judge Nahar

Yam is not moved   his face is unchanged
            He is not pressed

Kothar lays out *two* clubs
        tells their names:

                    "Your name
                    you are
                    AYAMUR   (Presser)

                    Presser
                    press Yam
        Press Yam from his seat   Nahar from his throne
        Whirl in Baal's hand   an eagle between his fingers
        Hammer Royal Yam
                    Judge Nahar   on the head
                                          between the eyes
            Yam will tumble   fall to the ground"

The club whirls   in Baal's hand
            an eagle   between his fingers
        hammers   the head of Royal Yam
                                 between Judge Nahar's eyes

Yam tumbles   falls to the ground
His face falls   he is moved

Baal drags Yam   lays him out
        ready to finish off Judge Nahar

"Slow down"   Athtart calls
"Shame"   she cries to Aliyan Baal
"Shame"   to Cloud Rider

"Royal Yam   is our prisoner
  Judge Nahar is our prisoner"

Baal is shamed at the word of her mouth

THE BATTLE BETWEEN MOT AND BAAL

A Ugaritic tale. Text: Gordon, *Ugaritic Textbook,* Text 49 VI.

MOT laments: (Death?)

> "My brothers   my mother's sons
>   Baal makes
> my enemies   my killers"

He returns to Baal in the Northern Close
   lifts his voice
   shouts again:

> "My brothers   my mother's sons
>   Baal makes
> my enemies   my killers"

They circle at each other
                           like stags

            Mot fierce
            Baal fierce

They gore each other
                           like buffalo

            Mot fierce
            Baal fierce

They bite each other
                           like snakes

            Mot fierce
            Baal fierce

They trample each other
                           like running beasts

Mot fallen
Baal fallen

From on high ŠAPAŠ   (Sun)
cries to godson Mot:
                    "Hear me:

                    You set yourself
                    against Aliyan Baal?
                    How?

                    As Bull EL   (God)
                    your father
                    hears you
                    he will uproot
                    your house base
                    he will overturn
                    your kingly chair
                    he will break
                    your judgment stick"

Godson Mot   fears
El's dear brave   takes fright

                    . . .

    (Baal is made king)

THE BATTLE BETWEEN ANAT AND THE
FORCES OF MOT

A Ugaritic tale of Anat's battle for her brother Baal. Text:
Gordon, *Ugaritic Textbook,* 'nt II.

> The Virgin Anat
> Camouflages her divine aura
> And puts on

The smell of goats and rabbits

She closes both the doors
Of the Palace of Anat

She catches up to the troops
In the mountain's slit

> In the valley
> Between the cities
> How she slays them!:

She cleaves the Shore folk
She smashes the Western man.

> All around her

Heads—a swarm of locusts
Hands—like crickets, as many
Soldiers' hands as thorns on cactus

> Anat bundles up her
> Prize

She loads up the heads
On her back:
She ties the hands
On her belt.

> And, returning from
> The valley

Her knees slosh through
The soldiers' blood,
The soldiers' flesh
Up to her hips.

She prods the captives
With the back of her bow.

And Anat comes home
Unsatisfied with her slaughters
In the valley.
She fights on, indoors.

She sets up

Chairs for soldiers
Tables for soldiers
Stools to be soldiers.

How she slays them!:

She smites them, then
Stands back
Her liver full of laughter
Her heart filled with joy
Overjoyed
For her knees wade in
Soldiers' blood:
Soldiers' flesh
Up to her hips.

When she has finished
Fighting in the house
Lunging between the tables

She is full

And she rubs her hands
In the soldiers' blood.

She pours the rich oil
Into a basin

And she washes
Her hands

Virgin Anat
Washes
Her fingers

The Sister-of-the-Peoples
Washes
Her hands in the blood
Of the soldiers
Her fingers in the gore
Of the soldiers

The chairs are only chairs again
The tables, tables
The footstools, footstools

                            She pours out water

To wash
In the dew of the heavens
In the oil of the land
The rain from Cloudrider.

The Heavens' dew
Bathes her.

                            The rain bathes her.

THE BATTLE BETWEEN ANAT AND MOT

A Ugaritic tale of Anat's battle in which she avenges her
brother Baal. Text: Gordon, *Ugaritic Textbook,* Text 49 II.

ANAT yearns for him   (Skylady?)
                    the heart of a cow for her calf
                    the heart of a ewe for her lamb
                    the heart of Anat for Baal

She catches Mot by a tear in his clothes
    grabs him by the edge of his sash
She raises her voice
    calls:
                        "You
                        Mot
                        Give back my brother!"

Godson Mot answers the Virgin Anat:
            "What do you want from me?

                    I was wandering
                    Walking through all the mountains
                        into the very liver of the earth
                            through every hill
                        into the very liver of the land

                    My breath   to man
                            was lost
                    my breath   into the noise of earth

                    I came to the pleasant land of Dabr
                    to the beauty of the fields of Šiḫlememat

                    I ran into Aliyan Baal

I put him in my mouth
                    like a lamb
                    like a kid
I chewed him up

The torch of the gods   Šapaš
glowed in the sky
                    at godson Mot's handiwork"

Day has passed after day
days have become months
Anat yearns for him
                    the heart of a cow for her calf
                    the heart of a ewe for her lamb

                    the heart of Anat for Baal

She catches godson Mot   slices him with a sword
                                tosses him in a sieve
                                scorches him in fire
                                grinds him with millstones
                                plants him in fields
                    so birds may eat him
                        sparrows eat his little bits
                        flitting from bit to bit

THE BUILDING OF BAAL'S PALACE

This Ugaritic text is included in this volume because Baal's palace is the earth in microcosm, as are temples. Text: Gordon, *Ugaritic Textbook*, Text 51 IV–VI.

(Athtart speaking):

> "He calls to Athtart   and her sons
>   to the goddess
>   and all her offspring
>
> 'Look
> there is no house for Baal
> as the gods have
>   no court
> as Athtart's sons have
>
> El's home is a shelter for his son
>
> the home of Lady Athtart of the sea
> is a home
>   for the untouched brides:
>   Pidraya's home
>   the daughter of light
>   Talaya's home
>   the daughter of rain
>   the home of Artsaya
>   the daughter of Y'bdr.' "

El   of the gentle heart says:

> "Am I to be an agent of Athtart
>   carrying hods?
>
> If Athtart will be a slave
>   making bricks
> a house will be built for Baal
>   as the other gods have
> a courtyard
>   fit for a son of Athtart"

Lady Athtart of the sea says:

        "Lord of the gods in wisdom
         your gray beard has taught you

        Now again Baal keeps rain season
                   mud season
              gives his voice in the clouds
              lets lightning loose to earth

        He will make whole a house of cedar
        He will erect a house of bricks

        The word shall be taken to Aliyan Baal:

     'Call the carpenter to your house
        the bricklayer inside your palace

      The mountains will crop you much silver
      the hills   beautiful gold
      the mines will crop you lapis

      So build a house of silver and gold
        a house of lapis jewels' "

Virgin Anat is happy   her feet thump the ground
She sets her face   at once   for Baal at Northheight
across a thousand fields   many many measures

Virgin Anat laughs
      lifts her voice
      shouts:
          "Be told   Baal   your telling   I bring you

          a house will be built for you
                   like your brother's
        a court
               like your kin's

Call the carpenter to your house
    the bricklayer inside your palace
The mountains will crop you much silver
the hills   beautiful gold

Build a house of silver and gold
    a house of lapis jewels"

Aliyan Baal is happy
He calls the carpenter to his house
    the bricklayer inside his palace
The mountains crop him much silver
the hills   beautiful gold
the mines crop him lapis

He sends for Kothar wa-Khasis

When Kothar wa-Khasis comes
he sets an ox in front of him

a fatling before his face
A seat is set
he sits   at Aliyan Baal's right
while they eat   and drink

Then Aliyan Baal says:

        "A house in a hurry   Kothar
        A palace rising fast

        Build a house quickly
        Raise a palace fast
            in the middle of Northheight
        The house will be on a thousand fields
        the palace   many many measures

Kothar wa-Khasis says:
        "Hear   Aliyan Baal
        and consider   Cloudrider

        I'll set a window in the house
            a window in the side of the palace"

Aliyan Baal says:

      "Do not set a window in the house
        a window in the side of the palace"

      (Because, apparently, Yam might use
        the window to get at Baal's "brides")

Kothar wa-Khasis says:

      "Again Baal what I say
      once more   the word of Kothar wa-Khasis:

      'Hear me   Aliyan Baal
      I'll set a window in the house
        a window in the side
        of the palace' "

Aliyan Baal says:

      "Do not set a window in the house
        a window in the side
        of the palace"

Kothar wa-Khasis says:

      "You will hear my word again   Baal"

His house is being built   palace raising

He goes to Lebanon for its trees
    to Siryon for its beautiful cedars

He sets fire in the house
    flames in the palace

So the first day and the second

          fire eats in the house
          flames   in the palace
   the third and fourth days
          fire eats in the house
          flames   in the palace
   the fifth and sixth days
          fire eats in the house
          flames   in the palace
Then on the seventh day

          fire leaves the house
          flames   the palace

Silver is made into tiles
Gold is made to bricks

Aliyan Baal is happy:
"I built my house of silver
my palace of gold"

Baal prepares his house
HADD   (Baal)
prepares his palace:
He slaughters cattle and sheep
kills bulls and fatlings
rams and calves of one year
lambs and kids

He calls his brothers into his house
his kin   inside his palace
He calls the seventy sons of Athtart

He fills
the ramgods with wine
He fills
the ewe-goddesses with wine
He fills
the oxgods with wine
He fills
the cow-goddesses with wine
He fills
the thronegods with wine
He fills
the throne-goddesses with wine
He fills
the gods with jugs of wine
He fills
the goddesses with vats of wine

All the time the gods   eating and drinking
                    the breast-suckers making happy

                    a salted knife and a slice of fatling
                    drinking wine from a cup
                              treeblood from a golden cup

YHVH'S BATTLE WITH THE SERPENT

These Canaanite-Hebrew texts, c. 1500 B.C., are remnants of a Canaanite myth contained within the Hebrew Bible. Text: Kittel, *Biblia Hebraica*.

Is. 51:9–10

Waken
Waken
Gird might of arm
YHVH
Waken as before endless generatings

Didn't you crush Rahab?
            hole Tannin?
Didn't you dry up Yam?
            mighty waters of Tehom?
                set the ⎰YAM deeps a path for the saved to tread?
                      ⎱sea

Job 26:12–13

In his might he stirred the ⎰sea
                          ⎱YAM
Then in his cunning crushed Rahab
By his wind set ⎰YAM in net
                ⎱sea
His hand made holes in the twisty snake

Ps. 74:13–17

You broke up ⎰YAM in your might
             ⎱sea
You smashed Tannin-heads in the water
You crushed Leviatan heads
Made him food for desert folk

You split spring and creek
You dried up   mighty rivers
The ⌠day is yours
    ⌡yom
The night is yours
You set up light and sun
You determined earthbounds
Summer and winter
                    you made them

Ez. 29:3–6a

"See me
I overcome you Pharaoh king of Egypt
                great Tannin squatting in the middle of its rivers
                    saying: 'My Nile. I made it.'

I put hooks in your cheeks
    stick the fish of your Nile to your scales
I drag you up from the middle of your Nile
                with all the fish of your Nile stuck on your scales
I throw you out on the desert
                you and all the fish of your Nile

You fall upon the field
You will not be brought to burial
                        but I give you
to the earthlife and skybird for eating

So all the Egyptians may know that I am YHVH"

Ez. 32:2–8

"The lion of nations you think yourself
    You are like Tannin in the sea:
            You tear up your rivers
            You churn the water with your feet
                muddy the rivers

This is what YHVH says:
      'I spread my net upon you
                      and a group of many peoples
     I drag you up in my snare
       throw you out on the land
       cast you on the field
       settle all the skybird on you
       stuff all the earthlife with you
       put your flesh on the hills
       fill the valleys with your carcass
       water earth with your flow
                  from your blood
       the channels will be full of you

     I will extinguish you by covering the skies
                   darkening the stars
     I will cover the sun in cloud
           the moon will not light its light
     I will darken all the lights in the sky upon you
         and put darkness on your land'

The speech of Adonai YHVH"

THE PHOENICIAN ORPHIC THEOGONY
ACCORDING TO HIERONYMOS
AND HELLANIKOS

This Greek theogony, c. 500 B.C., is taken from a Phoenician source of c. 700–800 B.C. Text: Diels-Kranz, *Die Fragmente der Vorsokratiker,* Vol. 1.

Water and Lady Hyle

then she got tough: Earth

he cuts and scatters
she hugs and mingles

who came before them?
don't ask
you don't want to say the name

Water and Earth's child
"he-water-and-she-earth"
dragon snake
two heads bull and lion
in between a god (man) face

shouldering wings
called Chronos 'Olam the Timeless
and Heracles Mel-kart

to Chronos came Need
who is Nature
the Inevitable
without a body
stretching out her stick
to scratch in limits for everything

Chronos—Need
the man—woman
maker of everything

the three children of dragon snake Chronos:
knowing FireAir
boundless Gap   set in the middle
foggy NightPlace

inside his three Chronos laid Egg
or he made his three Egg

inside Egg
Male and Female
the seeds of everything

and the third an unembodied god
gold wings on his shoulders
his ribs bulls' heads
a huge dragon snake wearing his head
he can take the body of everything that lives

he is mind

Egg father

Male and Female power

who is the third of the third three?
First Born
Zeus Disposer
Pan All

EMPEDOCLES, FROM *NATURE*

Fragments from the Greek text by Empedocles, c. 500 B.C., which in turn was probably taken from a Near Eastern source, c. 800 B.C., via the Greek Orphics. Text: Empédocle: *Les Origines* (Bollack, ed.).

Origins

I speak in two

sometimes   one grows from many
sometimes   many splits from one

two   the birth of deathly life
two   the leaving off

birth   the union of all makes and kills
leaving off   strips and is stripped

when deathly life divides itself
exchanges never cease

sometimes   through Love everything grows into one
sometimes   through Hate everyone splits in two

when one splits once again
many are born but do not live forever

since this exchanging never ceases
they are always motionless in a circle

say it once
say it twice

I speak in twos

sometimes   one grows from many
sometimes   many splits from one

Fire and Water and Earth and the high unfilled measure of Air

Hate hated twice by the roots equals them
Love that's in them becomes their friend in length and width

mind, look at her
don't sit there eyes astounded

born in their bodies
men worship her

she makes them think of desire
doing what joins them in peace and friendship

so they call her JOYOUS JOINER
Gethosyné   Aphrodite

no one alive has ever seen her
because she swirls in their eyes

all the roots are equal
the same in birth and age

ruling with different honor
each according to their nature

time sails in a circle
each has a chance

nothing added to them
nothing taken away

always the same
equal in birth and age

if they should leave off without limit
everything would die

all this—what makes it grow?
where did it come from?

how should the roots leave off
since nothing is empty of them

always the same
equal in birth and age

running across each other
they make all things

so on so forth forever

I will tell you something else
everything that is born and dies
is not really born
does not really die
it only mingles and exchanges
what has already been
mingled and exchanged

people call this "birth"
I will use the same words
"birth" and "death"
since that is the custom

when Light and Air
mingle

to make the body of a man
or animal tree bird

people say "it has been born"

when men animals trees birds leave off
people say "it has died"

there is no birth
there is no death

only mingling exchanging
the already mingled and exchanged

birth and death
are names people use

I use them
because they do

but there is
no birth no death

you are a fool
if you think there is

this in the marvelous bending of the human body

sometimes   through Love
all the limbs unite
all the limbs that have a right to a body
at the peak of flowering life

sometimes   through Hate
all the limbs are dismembered
broken into pieces
by the Strifes smashers of life

this also happens to trees
fish who live under Water's roof
animals in the hills
even the tumbler pigeon
who walks on his wings

so on so forth forever

Love

clinging Love kisses

see the hot bright Sun everywhere

the immortals bathed in heat in thick light
the rain everywhere icy and black

from Earth
the gracious and solid
flow forth

coming together in Love
desiring each other

from all that was
all that is or
ever will be

trees leave

men and women and animals and birth and fish Water feeds
and the long-lived gods honored above all else

there is no death
their life is not forever

always the same
equal in birth and age

running through each other
making everything that is

the exchange the roots
mixing mingling bring

The Four Roots

the goddess says
"think of painters
they use the drugs of many colors
to make figures that look like real things
giving body to trees men women
to animals and birds
fish Water feeds
even the long-lived gods honored above all else

this is the origin of everything
that flowers without number by day"

the names of the four roots of everything

        ZEUS
        bright Air

        HERA
        mother Earth

        AIDONEUS
        homeless Fire

        NESTIS
        Water   who with her tears
                   waters life's well

time sails in a circle
each has a chance

losing itself in each other
growing according to their share

always the same
running across each other

born men and animals
trees birds fish

so on so forth forever

born hair leaf
thick bird feathers
horn scales on strong backs
tall tree perch in the sea

so on so forth forever

parts looking for bodies
heads without necks
suddenly sprouting in Earth like cabbages
naked arms shoulderless
eyes watching for sockets
monsters
roaming Earth
rolling feet shambling hands

born two faces two bodies
cattle man-prowed
men beeve-headed
half male half female
their bodies in shadow

sometimes   through Love the roots come together to make one
sometimes   through Hate the roots split to make many

grown into one
they are completely swallowed

knowing how to grow into one from many
to be many after one splits into two

this way they give birth
but their life is not forever

since they never cease mingling and exchanging
they are always motionless in a circle

Love	Harmony	Aphrodite
Hate	Strife	Neikos

when Strife reaches the bottom of the dyne
Love is born in the midst of the swirl
everything assembles there to be 'one and only'
not quickly
but one from one
one from another
deliberately
coming together
mingling and mixing
then the countless tribes of living things
flow forth

Strife holds up above
all who refuse mixing and mingling
alternating with those who do

for Strife has not yet retired perfectly
from the furthest rim of the circle
part of him remains
the rest escapes the body of Sphere

he retreats
soft Love's immortal attack pursues

suddenly the living are born to die
although they'd learned not to

when they mingle and exchange
the countless tribes of the living
flow forth
shaped to hold every body
wonderful to see

Air with his long roots enters Earth
Fire burns underground

A kiss unites everything in every part
radiant Sun   Earth   Sky   Sea

partly they live in the living
but their life is not forever

everything ripe for mixing mingling
Aphrodite matches
submitting to each other
they grow one

everything that is in two
split
in birth
in mixing and exchanging
in image set upon it
is enemy to itself
to everything else that is in two
they do not know how to join in Love
they are lonely sad
because Hate and Strife are twin fathers of their race

Sphere Cosmeg

Sphere rounded in Harmony's compact gloom
smooths himself
circling gloriously
in lonely joy
Sphere equal everywhere
entirely without limit
smooths himself
circling in lonely joy

two branches do not spring from his back
he has no feet no quick knees
no part of sex
he is Sphere
equal to himself
entirely without limit
no Strife or Quarrel in his body
when huge Neikos leapt up
inside Sphere Cosmeg
reaching out to rule

now that his time
had sailed around
he marked out his own path
replacing Sphere's fat circle
one after another
all the limbs of Sphere shook

Earth

Earth   the center of Sphere

she meets the other roots
Fire   Rain   bright Air

their equal
in age and birth

anchoring herself in Love's
tight harbors of accomplishment

sometimes   stronger in one thing
sometimes   weaker in another

from the roots blood and all forms
of flesh sprang

                    BAUBO
                    the wombs [of Earth]

in her smooth cunts
pleasant Earth received
two of the eight parts of NESTIS
                         gleaming Water
two from HEPHAISTOS
            Fire

they were born bones
the skeleton Harmony joined

you will see
in the crusty back of shellfish
in the trumpet mollusk
tortoise with his stone skin
how Earth lives on top of flesh

hedgehog bristles point up
men sprouted from Earth
like heads of lettuce

gentle Fire has a short-lived share of Earth
Air brings clouds
Sea   sweat of the Earth

Sun and Moon

you hardly ever see the rapid arms of the Sun

untroubled he
sends his light flashing back
toward Olympos

gathering his Fire
he sails a circle in the sky

turning around Earth
smoothly spinning
his borrowed light
like a wheel track
at the edge of a field

sending out arms
like darts

sweet Moon
empty-eyed blind Night

gentle Moon looks with Love
on the luminous circle
of the Sun her king

Sun's arm punches
her smooth face

he hammers her

throwing his fists like darts
you hardly ever see

owl-eye Moon scatters
Sun on Earth
darkening as much land
as her face covers

ambushing light
Earth makes night

Sun's shining body is veiled
you cannot see the hairy tribes of Earth or Sea

Men and Women

Fire
when he split in two
fashioned in the night
angular men
wailing women

whole born sketches of men
sprang up from earth
like head lettuce
half Heat half Water

Fire
eager to mate himself in them
lifted them to light

though they did not show
the lovely body of their limbs
and were without voice
man's mark

wrapped in sheepskin cauls

since men are born
in Earth's warmer wombs
they are darker than women
hairier   and have a cock

the human body's birth
is split between
the mother's and the father's

when a man's clear sperm leaves him
enters his wife
when she is cold
a female is born

Love

the divided meadows of Aphrodite
give life

Love   Friendship   Harmony

a kiss
her eyes serious

a knot binds two
two eyes see one

just as the juice of a fig
bolts white milk and rivets it

Aphrodite joins with bolts of Love
as wheat bound by Water makes bread

Water marries wine
she does not Love oil

yellow crocus' rays
meet and mingle in linen threads

desire steals over me
softening mixing
in the organs of my body

all that is thick inside
full of holes outside
receives a surplus of Water
from the hands of Love

after Love Watered Earth with rain
breathless she gave the bodies of the living
to homeless Fire for hardening

everything was in her hands
when it grew the first time

the Love-light in your soft eyes
threaded mine
two eyes see one

when you're going out on the road at night
you take a lamp
Fire against the evening storms
when winds blow
you raise the windscreen
to keep out the cold
but the light leaps over the lamp's rim
piercing night far as he can go
with unworn lance

this is how Love guards her storied Fire
locked in the body's membranes
she kindles him in a girl's glancing eyes
spinning a net of svelte linen of flesh
to protect the flame from Water's depths
that surround her pupil

but the light leaps over the rims of your eyes
piercing night far as he can go
with unworn lance

from the four roots
from the mixing and exchanging Air Fire Earth Water
grew the shapes and colors of all living things
Love joined in Harmony

from them she made
indestructible eyes

"everything feels
and has a share of thought"

from the roots
Love joined in Harmony
everything was made

through them
each thinks suffers rejoices

Earth sees Earth
Water Water
Air Air
Fire Fire
Love Love
Hate Hate

so on so forth forever

sweet fucks sweet
bitter plunges in and out of bitter
sharp cuts sharp
salt couples salt

so on so forth forever

turned toward what is before them
men's thought grows

come listen to me
understanding increases thought

thoughts spin on tides of blood
that ebb and flow
for that is where what people call thought is

blood around the heart
men's thought

everything breathes in and out
through bloodless pipes of flesh
stretched throughout the body

delicate furrows pierce the mouth
the surface of the skin
there blood pools
and Air cuts for himself
easy passage in and out

gentle blood sings in the veins
while it retraces its path
leaping back into the body's crevices
and the straight flow of Air enters
but when blood returns
Air breathes out

there are exhalations
from everything that has been born

dog's nose tracks
the slices of themselves
animals leave behind
breath from their paws
lingers in fresh grass

shadows darken the river bottom
your hollow eyes
because they are alike
see the black in caves

every thing partakes of breath smell and sight
longing to return to themselves in others

time sails in a circle

"everything that is born
feels and has a share of thought"

Natural Demonstration

Air makes the evergreen
fruitful all year long

tall olive trees lay eggs

pomegranates ripen late
running over with juice

Water from bark
steeped in wood
is wine

salt hardens
pushed back on itself
by the gleaming blows of the Sun

there are drugs
that overcome sickness and age

I have shown you all this
so you can test it

so you will master the unwearying winds
that spring up waste fields harrying Earth

that when you wish
call them back

to bring for men
after black rain
bright weather

after summer drought
make rain to feed the trees
as it falls from the skies

and bring back from hell
the life of the dead

HYMN TO PHANES WITH PROEM
FROM THE *ORPHIC ARGONAUTICA*

Stanza 1 is from the *Orphic Argonautica,* a Greek text from
the second century A.D., using materials from c. 800 B.C.
Stanza 2 is from the *Hymn to Phanes,* a Greek Orphic text,
c. third century A.D., which is a revision of an earlier hymn of
the sixth or seventh century B.C. The remainder of this selection
is from the *Orphic Argonautica.* All texts: Hermann, *Orphica.*

Lyre god Apollo
I will sing for you
a new song
I will reveal your terrible arrows
to all men everywhere
but especially to those
my rites have kept pure

When Time and wailing Need
split the ancient egg
out stepped Love the firstborn
fire in his eyes
wearing both sexes
glorious Eros
father of immortal Night
Phanes, god of Brightness
whom Zeus swallowed and brought back
Zagreus
Osiris
Dionysos
offer myrrh
Bull Shouter
laden with gold
Seed of gods and men
Priapos
Erikapeios
horned

clandestine
unnamed
Sounding Rusher
All Shining Slayer of Night in the eyes of men
everywhere on the pure oars of his wings
my lord
quick-glancing Reflector
Sparkler
Blessed Clever Ubiquitous
Go rejoicing in the completed acts of his name
In the countless wombs of Earth
Time brought forth Air
and the grim goddess Death
and the Strainers the Tighteners
who stay beneath boundless earth forever
because of what they did

Then Healer
and Mountain Mother
who fashioned Huntress Moon Queen
from relentless Sky Father son of Time

Have you heard of the mangling of Zagreus?
of the gods who lived on Mount Ida?
of MotherEarth who wandered in the great gulf
in search of her child to give us law?

the meaning of dreams

the reading of the signs

the star roads

the cleansings needed

atonement

satisfaction

the mountains of gifts the dead require

what I learned
when singing and playing
I followed the shadowy paths of hell
in search of love

when in Egypt
I gave birth to the stag
as I neared holy Memphis
and the round cities of Apis
the eddying Nile surrounds
where I was taught my secrets

you have learned all things unerringly from my heart
I have done it by sixes and sevens

now the gadfly leaves me
stinging and burning
my body learns from the unremitting sky

you will learn from my voice
all the things I concealed
from stubborn men
how the heroes and half gods
passed over into Peiria
and the steep sheer head of the Wet Country
praying that I would be their messenger
that I would guide the stroking of their oars
I the precursor of their return
in White Boat against the inhospitable nations
of rich and reckless people
against the claiming of their gold

I sail on the ship of the world

FROM HESIOD, *THEOGONY*

(THE VISION)

A Greek text, c. 600 B.C., taken from Hurrian-Hittite and
earlier Indo-European forerunners dating from before 2300
B.C. Text: Hesiod, *Theogony* (West, ed.).

children of Zeus
grant me song
of the gods who are forever
who were born out of Earth and star-lit Sky
dark Night and Salt Sea

speak tell me
how we were born the beginning
of the ground we walk on
rivers ponds lakes
sea without end swelling rushing
stars sending light
sky cupped overhead
gods born of them
the gods givers of good things
dividing wealth among themselves
honors titles a palace in the mountains
Olympos

Muses living in the houses of Olympos
who was first?

"Gap was first
then Earth the great chair with her immense teat

then Pit hard to see
deep in the wombs of Earth

                    next Love
                  loveliest of gods
             who unstrings the body
                    tames the heart
                    breaks the mind
                      whether god or man
                    within his heart

        the children of Gap were Gloom and Night
              whom Love joined
         their children were bright Air and Day

                    Earth's firstborn was star-lit Sky
                      a lover to cover her
                        equal in every particular

              he made her his chair
                the seat forever for the happy gods

    the children of Earth
              the long hills where nymphs roam
                    who sleep in thickets
              sterile sea 'without sweet union of love'
                because his salt will not make her fruitful
                    in his swelling rushing
         Earth sheltered Sky
                    their children were the Earth-born the Geagants
                tidal Ocean
           sons Koios and Krois and Hyperion and Iapetos
    daughters Theis fixer Rhea flow-er Themis setter
         Mnemosyné recaller Phoebé with a golden crown
                        Tethys lady of the deeps

           her youngest Kronos 'air large birds ride'
                    thinks in crooked ways
                  most feared of all her family
              for in his energy he hated his father

                the children of Earth
                    Wheel Eyes hearts of force
                    Thunder Lightning Thunderflash
    they gave Zeus thunder they made him the thunder bolt
            like all the gods in everything
        except for the one eye turning in their forehead
            wheeling in place between their two eyes

            the three sons of Earth and Sky
                never named proud Kottos Briareos Gyes
                    from their shoulders
                        hundred hands leap forth
                    upon each of their shoulders
                    fifty heads wag
                    upon their muscled bodies
                        out of their shoulders
                not according to nature
        unapproachable ungraspable in their strength
                hated and feared most of all
                    as soon as they were born

                as soon as his children were born
                    Sky hid them away
                he deprived them of light
        shoving them back deep into the wombs of Earth
                he went away and laughed

                    Earth crowded groaned
            she thought of something clever and ugly
            she made gray adamant
                    made a sickle of it
    made her children understand what she wanted done with it
                sorrowing in her heart
            she encouraged them
                    'pay him back for what he has done
                        he was first to hurt'
                this is what she said

                    they were afraid
                 none of them answered
but great Kronos who thinks around corners was not afraid
                    he spoke to his wise mother
                    'I shall do it
                 I shall finish it
                    I do not love my father
                    he was first to hurt'
           he spoke huge Earth shook with joy in her heart
                 she hid him in a place of ambush
     she put the sickle with jagged teeth in his hand
                    she showed him her plan

                    great Sky came
                 bringing night
           lying heavy on Earth in love and desire
           she opened receiving him
     their son stretched out his left hand from ambush
in his right he held the great sickle with jagged teeth
                 he chopped off his father's balls
                    he threw them to the wind behind him
           they flew away a bloody track in the air
                    which Earth enfolded
     in full time she gave birth to the strong Curses
                    and the great Titans
     full-armored bursting with light shaking long spears
              and the Meliads nymphs of the ash tree
                    all over boundless Earth

                    when his balls cut down by adamant
                        fell from boundless Earth
        onto high Sea
                    battered they swam open currents
            from that deathless flesh foam blossomed
                inside the pink flower a girl was born and grew
                    she passed by holy Cythera
        she came to Cyprus surrounded by water's flood
                    she stepped onto land
                    august lovely goddess
            grass sprung up under her tapered feet
    Aphrodite born of foam Cytheria the well-garlanded
            because she grew inside the bloody foam
                    because she passed near Cythera
            Cyprogene because there she was born
                    on Cyprus wave washed
                Philomedes because she loves Love's bone
    because she was born inside her father's balls
            Love walks with her
                    Desire follows

            as soon as she was born
                    she went right to the race of gods
    this is the honor she holds this is what they allotted her
            her share among men and deathless gods
                    young girls' talk
                    their laughter and sweet deceit
            delight pleasure lovemaking softness

            the sons great Sky fathered he cursed
                    calling them Titans the Strainers
        because he said they tightened and strained
                    to do proud deeds
        and they would be paid back for it soon afterward"

FROM APOLLODORUS, THE *LIBRARY*
(GENEALOGICAL CATALOG)

A genealogical catalog from the Greek text by Apollodorus, c. third century B.C.–first century A.D., taken from a pre-Hesiodic source in Greek, which was derived from earlier Indo-European sources. Text: Apollodorus, *Bibliotheca* (Frazer, ed.).

Ouranos was first king of the ordered world
he married Gea

their first children were the Hundred-handed
        Briareus
        Gyes
        Kottos
they were impossibly big and strong
they had a hundred hands a hundred heads

their next children were the Cyclops
        Arges
        Steropes
        Brontes
each had one eye in the middle of their forehead
Ouranos tied them up and threw them into Tartaros
a dark place in Hades as far from earth
as earth is from sky

their next children were the Titans
        Okeanos
        Koios
        Hyperion
        Kreios
        Iapetos
        Kronos youngest of all

their daughters were the Titanides
            Tethys
            Rhea
            Themis
            Mnemosyné
            Phoebé
            Dioné
            Theia

Gea wept because Ouranos destroyed their children
he tied them up and threw them all into Tartaros
Gea persuaded the Titans to fight their father
she gave Kronos a sickle of adamant
all the Titans except for Okeanos fought Ouranos
Kronos cut off his balls and threw them out to sea

from the drops of his blood the Erinyes were born
            Alecto
            Tisiphoné
            Megaira

the Titans took away their father's kingship
they freed their brothers from the dark place of Tartaros
they gave the kingship to Kronos

Kronos tied them all up and threw them again into Tartaros
he married his sister Rhea

Ouranos and Gea told him
a son of his would take away his kingship
he swallowed his children as soon as they were born

he swallowed his first child
            Hestia

he swallowed
            Demeter
            Hera
            Pluto
            Poseidon

Rhea was enraged
she went to Crete carrying Zeus
she gave birth to him in a cave of Dicté
she gave him to the Kouretes to protect
to the brides Adrasteia and Ida to nurse
the brides fed him milk of Amaltheia
the Kouretes guarded the cave
banging swords on their round shields
so Kronos would not hear the voice of his child
Rhea wrapped a stone in baby blankets
and gave it to Kronos to swallow
she said it was Zeus

when Zeus grew up
he took Metis daughter of Okeanos to help him
she gave Kronos a drug to swallow
it made him throw up the stone
then the children he had swallowed

Zeus fought Kronos
his brothers and sisters helped
Gea said Zeus would win
if all those Kronos threw into Tartaros helped
Zeus killed their jailer Kampé
he smashed their chains

the Cyclopes gave Zeus thunder lightning and the thunder bolt
they gave Pluto a helmet Poseidon a trident

the children of Kronos used their weapons
they beat the Titans
they defeated their father
they tied them up and threw them into Tartaros
they chose the Hundred-handed to guard them

they threw lots for the kingship
Zeus won the kingdom of the sky
Poseidon the kingdom of the sea
Pluto the kingdom of Hades

Zeus married Hera
their children were
    Hebé
    Eileithuia
    Ares

Zeus fucked many goddesses and many girls

his daughters by Themis daughter of Ouranos were the Horai
    Eirené
    Eunomia
    Diké

also the Moirai
    Klotho
    Lachesis
    Atropos

his daughter by Dioné was Aphrodité

his daughters by Eurynomé daughter of Okeanos were the Graces
    Aglaia
    Euphrosyné
    Thaleia

his daughter by Styx was Persephoné

his daughters by Mnemosyne were the Muses
    Kalliope first
    then Kleio
    Melpomené
    Euterpé
    Erato
    Terpsichoré
    Ourania
    Thaleia
    Polymnia

THE SETHIAN CREATION STORY

The Sethian creation story according to Hippolytos, c. third century A.D. The Sethians were a Jewish Gnostic sect active in the first century B.C.–first century A.D. Text: Hippolytos, *Refutatio* (Wendland, ed.).

1. *the 3 of beginning: light, dark, spirit*

        spirit where light and dark void each other
clear and unconfounded
                no wind blowing gentle breeze
    ointment or perfume
                  it steals into things
                      better than words

       light above dark below spirit between

              light the sunray on dark beneath
        in molten fire everywhere incenses
              the subtleties of spirit
       to lead powers of both alive
  into dark whose fearful water drinks light
                in spirit essence
     thinks and thinks over
         if light leaves
she knows herself isolate
      invisible shrouded asleep heartless inert
        willing her to assemble within
              glints and chromes of light
              to the spirit's lifting

      (image:
        the eye's vitreous dark
        spirits light
          down its black hole)

                    patrolling for light
                        dark desires outward splendor to see
                            and bind his emissaries
                                freckling night sea
            light and spirit
                    empower themselves to stand
                            toward each other
                                    embracing
                                    plunging into dark
                                        the strong down water

2. *the seals*

                    all powers of the 3 of beginning
                                    number countlessly
                            thinking and thinking again
                                while alone they rest
            should a power close another
                        self lawed by difference to strike
                            this marks both
                                sealing stamped figures
            doing this over and over
                            forging endless seals
                    that type everything that lives

3. *womb*

                the first marking of the 3
                        coined womb
                            in character newly jammed open by cock
                    she the great seal of heaven and earth
                            circling midway omphalos
                                    the navel stone
                        (counterpart:
                                any womb a child quickens
                            swallows a size of heaven
                                and earth
                                    sitting changelessly
                                        on cunt stool)

when earth and sky close in womb
              they seal the powers of the 3
        striking them off beyond number
           in body of wombs
        shredding into type
              tiles of light odors of spirit

4. *wind*

      from dark
        from water her oldest
           boisterous wind
        beginner who enforces all birth
       in sea foam
      turning out waves
         dances in them
        child shivering their wombs
   impelling man or mind
       to well up
        in the source of their coming forth
    taken as ocean is
         when spirit kicks
           showering headlong

    every wave wind tears from water
        and puts child into
      buds within power of woman of birth
  fleshing in the new life
     splintered light
      spirit stealth

5. *the god of this world*

     the new life this sunray of wave
       is a finished god
   generation bears down
       wind blows to birth his temple

woven in water
    he lights dark
        mixes and mingles in bodies
            salting them
fighting
    helpless to break the bonds of type
        no exit no liberty
            from the charnel house of womb
        broken spark
            slivered splinter star seed
        compacted in the reused bodies of many
        the voice of the lord is upon the waters
        the god of glory thunders
        the lord is upon many waters
schemes worries
        how to escape death
            and kill the dark sod body
        father wind who is below
            roaring and swelling
                stamped him with
          knocking up waves
         making the perfect mind of light
           his not-of-his-body son

god of this world
      wind child glancing from bright thought
          eye of spirit borne down in water
      churning in dark the torn cunted fear-bitter sea

6. *manchild*

    once wind has desired the waves in spirals out of ocean
        blowing within them
            power of women of generation
      their wombs swallow every kind and gender
            where light sticks
        so that whatever they strike
            barbs dark and is seen

the fury wind of night whirling strength in his fear
turns the hissing dyne snake
cyclone serpent daddy of birth
seals the whirled
marking everything at once
funneling light and spirit home
into the cruel disordered womb of curse
fathering there manchild
for the danced water womb
set of many waves
does not love or open for any strike of flesh
but snake's

7. *word*

to retell this story
the perfect word of light
in serpent's body beast
cheats the womb
coming as her cherished
disposed as her counterfeit the snake

fathered in womb's cloaked trench
by water's oldest the serpent/wind/beast
word breaks the chains that bind the mind
for *himself of no reputation he took upon himself*
the form of a servant and was made in the body of men
but not enough his journey down into a virgin's womb
laboring in that darkness
he must drink opening the door the womb's secret pain
and be washed *in the well of water*
springing up into everlasting life

THE NAASENE COSMOLOGY

This is a cosmology from the Ophites (Naasenes), a Jewish
Gnostic sect of snake-worshipers active from the first century
B.C. through the second century A.D. Text: Hippolytos,
Refutatio (Wendland, ed.).

1. Naas The Serpent Whom We Wear

you can   make   7   from the brain

vaulted room

wings   on either side
wind blows on

through blood pipes

to Pine Nut

down   Spine Sperm

tailing in cock cunt

where brain kern sleeps in secret blood

this is in small Serpent Naas   who made us

brain the dragon head
six other coiling lines from there
bind the corpse
spine   containing the well-head   the stinging tail
the seventh

2. Naas The Great Man

                                    "Who shall declare his generation?"
"Earth   mother   man   willing   a   good   gift
not   loving   the   wild   ones   only
but   devising   a
             thinking
             gentle
             and   lovely   one"   :
             Alalcomenes in Boeotia near Lake Cephisis
             Koros of Ida of Crete   branch of the gods
             Korybas of Phrygia   whom the sun first saw
                         jumping up like a tree from the mother
             Pelasgos from Arcadia   older than Moon
             Diaulos in Raria   mother: Eleusis the Free
             Kabiros of Lemnos   pretty Mystery child
             Alcyoneus from the Phlegaian Fields   oldest of the
                     big Earth—born   mother: Pallené
         Iarbas   desert child   Libya   chewing Zeus nuts
         Nile   making without fathermother
                 mud rendering the living corpse
                     buying meat from water
         Oan of Assyria
         Adam from Chaldea   whom Earth alone enwombed
Naas stared down into the statue pool of self so hard it moved
         said :
     LIVE   !   SUFFER   !   DIE
                 punishing   the slave image
                     over—mastered by what heshe saw
         The Great Man names the whole family of Earth and Sky
                     to where we struggle to escape

3. Soul

         What The Great Man did to the statue of many and single name
             is called
                         SOUL
             which makes all things and makes them grow

                        even stones
               for they undergo increase
                    accession
              the food that feeds us all
    Soul   a 3   and a 1
                        the names of soul
               according to the AsSyrians
                    :
                    Adonis
                    Endymion
                    (Attis)

soul Adonis
               Venus loves
                        and desires
               for she is natural increase

soul Adonis
               Koré or Persephone loves
                    then Adonis leaves Venus
                    and parts from generation

soul Endymion
               when Moon passes into love for him
                    desires to remove "above"
                        is demanded and
                        responds into life

when the mother of the gods cuts off the balls of Attis
                        yet loves him anyway
    it is because The Great Man has recalled the male from him
                    Adonis lives
               having surrendered the parts of earth
                    to the unconsummated world "above"
                    "where there is neither Jew nor Greek

               bond or free

               male or female :
               for all are one in Jesus Christ"

               a new man   a malefemale

4. "Above"

Lady Change   Mother of the Gods   is not alone
          Naas says and   Word agrees

                                     :

     "what you cannot see of The Great Man
             the world of creation does
        knowing   heshe is their author
            their undying power"
    "for the purpose of leaving them without excuse"

  the creatures that know do not thank him
          their hearts are emptied
     saying they are wise
          they become fools
  changing The Great Man in them to corpse man
  and birds and four-foot and crawling things

    so Great Man let them love one another
       each according to their self diminution
      the women stopped fucking
         the men left them

men playing with men   with the "unseemly" :
come   that first and happy substance
figureless   cause of all figures   that come into shape

    receiving in themselves the just payment for their mistakes

5. Logos Hermes

  :   Hermes   Cyllené's son   calls away the breath
     of those   who think back   on home
     in his hands   holds   a pretty golden   stick
        that soothes   the eye
          if he wants it   to
   but wakes   others   from death's sleep

with   the stick   makes passes   in the   air
their chirping breaths   churn   in answer   follow
into the   turns   of magic   cave like bats   children of   night
if one falls   from   shelving rock
                              the rest   stick together
like birds   the ghosts   in swirling flocks
              chase   the wand
across Earth's   broad   roads   over Ocean's springs
                    and   White Rock Leuké
past   Sun Gate   and the   country   of dreams
                                        perching in
                              fields of asphodel
              where   souls wait
pictures   of those who   have done their   work and   died   :

Hermes the Cock
                    master of life and death
who awakens the sleeping to a recollection of self
                    conveying The Great Man from "above"
         into   the   fiery creation of clay
                         to serve Ialdabaoth a 4
                         father of the formal world

Hermes the Christ
                    in all who have been generated
                    the figured Man Son
                    from figureless Logos

         in Eleusis   "Hyé : Kyé"
Rain ZeusBacchus :   Get Big With Baby

              when Ocean ebbs   then   :
                    a generation of men

         but flooding   towards the Wall and Fortress
                    of White Rock Leuké
              makes
                    a generation of gods

         Ocean Jordan dividing Israel from Egypt

THE NAASENE COSMOLOGY   331

6. Naas The Great Man (II)

Matters if
      you are   Titan   or   Zeus   or Lady Change   ?

Attis, dark tearing of the Mother of the gods
     whom   :
     AsSyrians call   —Adonis   longed-for 3 times
     Egyptians   —Osiris   Moon's sky horn
     Greeks   —   Sophia
     Samothracians   —   Adam
     Haemonians   —   Corybas
     Phrygians   —   PAPA or Corpse or God   or
            Fruitless or Green Wheat Kern
                   Reaped In Peace   or
            Amygdalos' Child
                   a man a musician

   I   want to sing to you, Attis, Lady Change's Son
         not with roaring trumpets
           skirling pipes of Ida of Crete
             that fit so well
              Kouretes' Chorus

     I will join my song with Apollo's   harp
           intoning

       EVAN ! EVOE !

     for you are Pan
       :   Bacchus
     herding the blinding stars

7. Naas The Serpent In The Garden

every one under heaven   : a temple/Naos of Serpent Naas
           anywhere you do a holy thing
              you enter   Naos   house of Naas

         you cannot leave the temple of yourself
             except to return to Naas

```
Naas    :    stream of Water    Ocean spring
                  horn of the one
                  one-horned bull
                  goring all in himherself
                      so that he gives them beauty and bloom
                          nature and peculiarity

Naas    :    River of Eden    dividing into four
                  Eden the brain
                          robed in seven : veils of
                                  Isis of generation
                          Paradise as far as the head

            but coming in and out

                  the four rivers

            :

            Pishon    surrounding the land    Havilath
                  where there is gold
                  gold of that land excellent
                  bdellium and the onyx stone
                      :
                  the eye
                  that by its colors
                          testifies to what is said
            Gihon    river of Ethiopia
                          tortured labyrinth

                  :

                  the ear

            Tigris    for Assyria
                  swift as breath    and smell of : nose
                  drawn and pushed forth in analogy

            Euphrates    :
                          mouth for praise for food
                          feeding and incorporating
                              The Great Man
                                  who is
                  "the water above the firmament"

        "  if you knew what to ask
              he would give you living bubbling water  "
```

into this water every breath enters choosing itself forming shape
                              peculiarity   desires   each nature
                                more than iron   the magnet
                              or gold the sea falcon's backbone
                                    and chaff   amber

        through Naas the blind man will see Paradise Park

                              planted with every tree
                              and fruit of the Tree

              water sighing through the trees and fruits

        will see from one and the same water

                              olive tree drink
                                    and draw oil
                              vine curve down
                                    and find wine
                              so on and so forth forever

        The Perfect Man is unknown in this world
                        betrayed by the ignorant
                    who are as a drop in a cask
                              small dust in the balance pan

        Pass through the third gate
                    receive the proof of things unseen
                        that who you are is all you are not

FROM OVID, *METAMORPHOSES*

From the *Metamorphoses* of Ovid, A.D. 9, from various earlier
sources. Text: Ovid, *Metamorphoses* (Proosdij, ed.).

before land was or sea or sky that covers all
nature everywhere wore the same face
which you might call "chaos" raw unformed mass
unharmonious ununion of the seeds of things
all crowded together into the same place
all at war with each other
all unaware
the sun gave no light
the moon did not lead out the months
earth did not spin in the void balanced by its weight
the ocean did not reach into the long shores of the land
though there was land and sea and sky
you could not walk or swim or look into air that lacks light
nothing knew form
all stumbled into each other
in one body they fought
cold with hot wet with dry soft with hard
that without weight with that which did
a god it was or must have been
or a kindlier nature who stopped this war
split land from sky sea from land
the gassy heaven from thick heavy air
freed them from blind chaos
bound them in their separateness by the concords of peace
each in its own place
the force of fire weightless form of arched heaven leapt up
made a place for itself in the sky's highest tower
next to fire air lay second in lightness and station
next earth thicker than fire and air
preserving the heavy elements
pressed down by its own weight
last of all water embracing solid earth flows around it

                    when he whichever god it was
had so arranged chaos
         reduced it divided it in sections into proper members
              he englobed earth a perfect sphere
                    so it would be equal in every part
         then ordered the sea to flow around it
              and swell into waves at the wind's blast
breaking on the shores of the encircled continents
                    to them he added springs swamps lakes
         ringed the rivers flowing down their steep banks
              and set them far apart from each other
                    partly absorbed by earth
                    the rest rushing into the sea
emptying into the plains of a freer water
                    where they stroke beach instead of riverbank
now he ordered the fields to widen out valleys to sink
the forests to cover in leaf in stone the mountains to rise up
              two zones divided the sky on the left
                    two on the right
              so the universe set and grew hard in its place
god thought caused it to divide into two
              the same number as before
and the same number of districts to be stamped on the earth
                    the one in the middle is too hot
              snow covers the two at the poles
         two others he put between the middle and the ends
              and gave them temperateness heat mixed with cold
                    overhead lies the air
              heavier than the zone of fire
         in the same proportion as water is than land
there he ordered mist and cloud to take their places
                    and thunder shaking men's minds
              and the winds that flash out in thunder bolts
the workman did not give them all the sky for their home
              but even now it is difficult to prevent them
                    from lashing out against the world
although they each blow in a different part
                    such is their fraternal discord

the East Wind went off to the kingdom of dawn
to Nabataea and the mountains of Persia
made bright by the rays of Matin
the West Wind combs the land evening where the sun sets
the bristling North Wind sweeps through Scythia and the Northland
the country directly opposite
is made continually wet by the clouds of the rainy South Wind
over them he laid hazy air lacking weight
showing no trace of earthen dung
he had hardly separated things into their fixed orbits
when the stars blocked by blind mist
grew to shining through the sky
so that no place in the universe would be without its own form of life
stars and god shapes peopled the heavenly earth
water made a home for silvery fish
land sheltered the animals
air fit for flying the birds
a living thing holier than all these capable of higher mind
to be master of all was as yet lacking
Man
whether the workman created him from divine seed
a race from a better world
whether the fresh earth just separated from the lofty fire
preserved some fragments of heaven
which Prometheus mixed with rain water
molding it in the likeness of the gods who rule over everything
is unknown
in any case Man came into existence
while all other living things down cast stare at the ground
he gave man a high face
told him to look up at the sky to lift his head to the stars
this is how the universe which only moments before
had been unformed without image
changing aspect took upon itself form and forms strange till then

FROM OVID, *FASTI*

From the *Fasti* of Ovid, A.D. 16, taken from native Italian
sources. Text: Ovid, *Fasti* (Frazer, ed.).

January First the Calends

dawn
the senate and people unlock his temple

sky burns with new fire
saffron sparkles on the fire place
flame beats on the temple's gold—new-won splendor

kind words now
no arguing—look what it did before

in untarnished white the procession moves towards the hill
wearing the color of the day

new rods of office
new purple on their cloaks
who's that sitting on the ivory chair—never saw him before

priests stretch the cow's neck

ax falls

Janus alone looks back

flooding the room with light
two heads two faces
staff in his right hand
key in his left

the mouth facing front speaks

"long ago they called me Chaos
that's how old I am

fire air earth water were one

argument split them
fire went up

air in the middle

earth and water sank down

all found new homes

then I
up 'til then Sphere
shape without image
took on face and body of a god

now just to remind you I was Chaos
I look the same back and front

there's another reason—listen

whatever you see—sky sea clouds land
I open and close with my hand
I guard/regard the world
law of the wheeling hinge is mine
I unlock war and peace
I sit in front of the gates of heaven
with the kindly Hours
Day-Father comes and goes
I meter him

priests feed me cookies of barley and spelt
mixed with salt
call me funny names Opener Closer
but that's the way it is
every door has two sides
one facing the people
the other the Lar inside

porter of heaven's door I see East and West
who goes in and out

Hecaté has three faces
so she can watch three roads meet
me too—so I won't waste time
I look two ways without turning"

"why does the year begin in winter?

why not in spring

flowers

time made new

vines puffed out
tree fingering her green hems
wheat bearding earth
birds twittering winnowing air
cattle living it up out in the fields
then sunlight is sweet
swallow returns
builds her nest of clay
under the roof beam

plow sow do it all again
why not then?"

"in two words: winter sunstill—one sun ends another begins
Phoebus and the new year start up together"

FROM VERGIL, ECLOGUE #6

From Eclogue #6 by Vergil, c. late first century B.C., is taken
from Hellenistic and Roman sources, c. 400 B.C. or later.
Text: Vergil, *Omnia Opera* (Papillon and Haigh, eds.).

Forward, Muses

the boys Chromis and Mnasyllus slunk into Silenus' cave
where they found him sleeping off a drunk
veins overblown by wine
garlands in petal flakes all around him
his well-worn drinking cup snoozing in one hand
                    dangling by the handle

he'd promised them the song of the making of the world
but hadn't made good his word

so they chained him up
Aeglé helped
            (ah Aeglé, prettiest of them all)
she painted the top of his head
with blood red mulberries while he watched

"let me go, fellas,
you'll get your song
and later on
she'll get hers"

        then he sang
and then you would have seen Fauns and every wild thing
dance to the numbers in his voice
the stiff oak swaying her top

"the seeds that flower earth, wind and sea
            water as well as fire
                    drove through the great void
from these primes
        everything began
        the soft circle of world

                    grew together
            farmland hardened
                    locking at sea the Sea Father
        the pretty shapes of things taking form
                            bit by bit
        rain falling clouds jammed together overhead
                now the first time   woods spring
                        here and there
                    beasts roamed the unknowing hills"

    and then he sang about us
        born from the stones Pyrrha   threw over her shoulder
        Italians living in Italy Saturn's golden land

    and then about the vulture in the Caucasus
                        who bites Prometheus in his passion
                        because he stole god fire

Appendix

Numerical Creation Texts

(SCHOOL OF) PYTHAGORAS,
THE WORLD OF NUMBERS

These Greek stories dating from the seventh–sixth century B.C. were part of the teachings of the school of Pythagoras and were collected by various ancient writers. The fragments used are numbered as follows: 1. Galen, *Historia Philosophica*, in Diels, *Doxographi Graeci;* 2. Aetius, *Placita* II 63–65, in Diels; 3. Philolaus, fragment 12, in Diels-Kranz, *Die Fragmente der Vorsokratiker;* 4. Parmenides, fragment 37, in Diels-Kranz; 5. Aristotle, *De caelo* II.13; 293a 19; 6. Aetius, in Diels-Kranz, Vol. I, 454 41ff.; 7. Aristotle, *Metaphysics* I.5; 8. Aetius, *Placita* I 3 8, in Diels; 9. Aristotle, *Physics* IV.6; 10. Aristotle, *Metaphysics* XII.6; 11. Aetius, *Placita* I 7 18, in Diels; 12. Aristotle, *Metaphysics,* 1.5; 13. Hippolytus, *Philosophumenon* 2.3–.18, in Diels; 14. Hermias, *Irrisio Gentilium Philosophorum* 16, in Diels; 15. Aristotle, *Nichomachean Ethics* II.5.

1.   —3 D—
                    the numbers
             as Pythagoras proposed them

                          out of the cube
                                earth
                    out of the pyramid
                                fire
                    out of the octahedron (* * *)
                                water
                    out of the dodecahedron
                                the Sphere of all

2.   *or*

                    out of the octahedron
                                air
                    out of the icosahedron
                                water
                    out of the dodecahedron
                                Sphere

3.   there are five of Sphere
                earth fire water air inside
             Sphere the barge makes five

4.   at the center (of Sphere)
                   Fire

5.   Guard of Zeus
                the daimon of direction
                  who holds the keys
               Right and Need

4.   Earth star
            circles Guard

        for Night and Day

6.   now the nature of number is ten
  everybody counts to ten
           and then goes back to   one

7.   so there are ten stars
                but you only see nine
        the tenth the counter-earth you cannot see
          (it is always behind Guard?)

8.   number makes

9.   empty cuts

10.   #1
        the only one

11.   #1 the god
                       who is the birth of 1

                   #2 the uncertain the aorist
                       the evil

12.   the 2's which are ten

1	2
end	endless
odd	even
one	many
right	left
male	female
stop	go
straight	bent
light	dark
good	bad
square	elongated

               pairs begin

13.   number is first
            the aorist the unholdable
                   that holds all numbers in endless
            numbers down to many

Pythagoras was four
before he was five

1. Aithalides pilot of the *Argo*
2. Euphorbos who fought at Troy
3. Mermotimos the Samian
4. Pyrrhos the Delian
5. Pythagoras

so   you do not die
you leap from one to another

what did Pythagoras   learn from Zaratas the Chaldean?

"daddie and mommie did it

he is light
she is shadow

| warm | dry | light | fast | daddie |
| cold | wet | heavy | slow | mommie |

the world is sexed in two's

harmony

sun's circle is music

two gods

sky demon   who is fire   sharing air warm and cold
earth demon   who is water   (sharing sweet and salt?)

one makes heaven grow
the other earth

#1	fathernumber	
#2	woman	even
#3	male	odd
#4	female	even

all numbers are fours

which makes ten the completed number

$$1 \quad + \quad 2 \quad + \quad 3 \quad + \quad 4 \quad = \quad 10$$

holy tetraktys

'spring of the roots
of timeless birth'

. . .

the fours of ten
completed number
are
1. number
2. monad
3. power
4. cube

interlacing 'mixing and mingling'

power	×	power	=	powerpower
power	×	cube	=	powercube
cube	×	cube	=	cubecube

and so on

until there are all numbers
fathermothering everything

but only seven shapes

number   monad   power   cubepowerpowerpowercubecubecube

don't worry   —can't hurt you or get you dirty

they are you
and everything else

don't forget
    don't eat beans

why?
—listen

when the world was born
so was the bean

how can you   tell?

if you chew a bean until it's pulp
then put it under the sun for a while
it'll smell like come

a better way of finding out—

take a bean when it's blooming
put it and its flower in a jug
bury for a few days

know what you'll find?

a womb in the jar
a baby's head inside"

. . .

Pythagoras also said

"stay quiet"

he made them stay in little rooms
underground

14.

FIRE $=$ 24 $+$ 4

1 $=$ 6 $\longrightarrow$

AIR $=$ 48 $+$ 8

$\longrightarrow$ $+$ 8

WATER $=$ 128 $+$ 20

$\longrightarrow$ $=$ 120

AITHER $=$ 12 $\longrightarrow$

EARTH $=$ 6 $\longrightarrow$

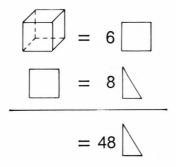

$$\square = 6 \,\square$$

$$\square = 8 \,\triangle$$

$$= 48 \,\triangle$$

15.   I give   you give   that is justice

A Greek text, c. third century A.D., drawn from Egyptian sources, c. third–fourth century B.C. Text: Hippolytos, *Refutatio* (Wendland, ed.).

$$
\begin{array}{c}
\text{one} \\
\#1 \\
+1: \\
2 \\
+1: \\
3 \\
+1: \\
4 \\
\hline
10
\end{array}
$$

10—beginning number: ending it as well—   1

		10	=	1		
10	×	10	=	100	=	1
100	×	10	=	1000	=	1
1000	×	10	=	10000	=	1

the atomic
numbers: 3   5   7   (9(

7 = the orbit of 6 days plus 1

2
4
8 kindred

according to position
and division

```
                    1    =    Fire
                    2    =    Air
                    3    =    Water
                    4    =    Earth
```

god made the   world   a malefemale

fire and air   halfsphere of 1

blissful   rising   male

water and earth   halfsphere of 2

girlish   wanton   willful

fire and air   in 1

male and female

make the diacosm grow

```
                fire    :    male
                air     :    female
```


but look at this :

```
                water    :    male
                earth    :    female
```

therefore :

```
            fire    powers    air
            water             earth
```

. . .

subtract   9
    from any number—they will end properly
                    some in 1—male
                    some in 2—female

$$\bigcirc \quad = \quad 360'$$
$$= \quad 40 \times 9$$

1	2
Fire	Air

$$= \quad 4 \times 90$$
$$= \quad 360'$$

3	4
Water	Earth

$$= \quad \bigcirc$$

light $=$ 1

dark $=$ 2

" and life to light, according to nature, and death to the duad
and to life, justice; and to death, injustice "

therefore : whatever the male numbers
produce is good

but the children of
female numbers
are mischievous

example :

361 — 9's $=$ 1

605 — 9's $=$ 2

you can compel   each number to reveal its reverted function

Selected Bibliography

Texts (many with commentary and translation into some modern language)

1. J. Burnet, *Early Greek Philosophy*.
2. R. H. Charles, *The Apocrypha and Pseudepigrapha of the Old Testament*.
3. G. Friedlander, *Pirke de Rabbi Eliezer*.
4. Th. Gaster, *Thespis*.
5. H. L. Ginsberg, *The Legends of Canaan*.
6. H. G. Güterbock, *The Song of Ulikummi*.
7. R. Haardt and J. F. Hendry, *Gnosis, Character and Testimony*.
8. A. Heidel, *Babylonian Genesis*.
9. Hesiod, *Theogony*, N. O. Brown (ed.).
10. J. Pritchard, *Ancient Near Eastern Texts*.
11. N. Sandars, *Poems of Heaven and Hell from Ancient Mesopotamia*.
12. E. A. Speiser, *Genesis* (in the Anchor Bible).

Secondary works

1. W. F. Albright, *Yahweh and the Gods of Canaan*.
2. M. Astour, *Hellenosemitica*.
3. V. Bérard, *Did Homer Live?*
4. The Cambridge Ancient History, Third edition, Vols. 1–4.
5. E. Dhorme and R. Dussaud, *Les anciennes religions orientales* (11).
6. C. Doria, "Introduction to the Phoenician History" (in *Io, #6*).

7. ———, "The Dolphin Rider" (in Macintyre [ed.], *Mind in the Waters*).
8. ———, "Commentary to Justin's *Baruch*" (in *Panjandrum*, #8).
9. ———, "Commentary on *Enoch*" (in *Io*, #21).
10. M. Eliade, *The One and the Two*.
11. A. Erhardt, *In the Beginning*.
12. H. Frankfort, *The Intellectual Adventure of Ancient Man*.
13. ———, *Ancient Egyptian Religion*.
14. K. Freeman, *The Pre-Socratic Philosophers*.
15. C. Gordon, *Homer and the Bible*.
16. W. C. Guthrie, *Orpheus and Greek Religion*.
17. E. Havelock, *Preface to Plato*.
18. P. Houwink Ten Cate, *The Luwian Population Groups of Lycia and Silicia Aspera During the Hellenistic Period*.
19. E. O. James, *The Tree of Life*.
20. ———, *Creation and Cosmology*.
21. S. N. Kramer, *Mythologies of the Ancient World*.
22. S. Moscati, *The Face of the Ancient Orient*.
23. C. Olson, "A Century or So Before 2000" (in *Maximus IV, V, and VI*).
24. R. Patai, *The Hebrew Goddess*.
25. ——— and R. Graves, *Hebrew Myths*.
26. M. Ramnoux, *La nuit et les enfants de la nuit*.
27. G. Scholem, *Jewish Gnosticism, Merkabah Mysticism and Talmudic Tradition*.
28. M. L. West, *Early Greek Philosophy and the Orient*.